D0282743

CRIMES OF ART + TERROR

Frank Lentricchia + Jody McAuliffe

The University of Chicago Press Chicago + London

FRANK LENTRICCHIA is the Katherine Everett Gilbert Professor of Literature and Theater Studies in Trinity College of Arts and Sciences at Duke University. He is the author or editor of ten critical works, most recently *Modernist Quartet*, several novels, and a memoir.

JODY McAULIFFE is associate professor of the practice of Theater Studies and Slavic Languages and Literatures at Duke University. She is a director, a fiction writer, and the editor of *Plays, Movies, and Critics*.

The University of Chicago Press, Chicago 60637
The University of Chicago Press, Ltd., London

Printed in the United States of America

12 11 10 09 08 07 06 05 04 03 1 2 3 4 5
ISBN: 0-226-47205-1 (cloth)

Library of Congress Cataloging-in-Publication Data

Lentricchia, Frank.
Crimes of art + terror / Frank Lentricchia + Jody McAuliffe.
p. cm.
Includes bibliographical references and index.
ISBN 0-226-47205-1 (cloth : alk. paper)
1. Literature, Modern—19th century—History and criticism. 2. Literature, Modern—20th century—History and criticism. 3. Literature, Experimental—History and criticism. 4. Avant-garde (Aesthetics) I. McAuliffe, Jody, 1954– II. Title.

PN761 .L46 2003
809′.911—dc21

2003006545

♾ The paper used in this publication meets the minimum requirements of the American National Standard for Information Sciences—Permanence of Paper for Printed Library Materials, ANSI Z39.48-1992.

FOR MAEVE LENTRICCHIA, JACK McAULIFFE,
ELAINE HAYNES, AND STANLEY KAUFFMANN

About the middle of the sixteenth century there lived beside the banks of the River Havel a horse-dealer called Michael Kohlhaas, the son of a schoolmaster, who was one of the most honourable as well as one of the most terrible men of his age. Until his thirtieth year this extraordinary man could have been considered a paragon of civil virtues. In a village that still bears his name he owned a farm where he peacefully earned a living by his trade; his wife bore him children whom he brought up in the fear of God to be hard-working and honest; he had not one neighbour who was not indebted to his generosity or his fair-mindedness; in short, the world would have had cause to revere his memory, had he not pursued one of his virtues to excess. But his sense of justice made him a robber and a murderer.

HEINRICH VON KLEIST, *MICHAEL KOHLHAAS*

CONTENTS

INTRODUCTION

In his elegiac meditation on the Easter Insurrection of 1916, W. B. Yeats broods on the recasting of the educated of privileged class provenance into violent actors, in an Irish political drama designed to throw off colonial oppression. Yeats is enthralled with the transformation of the respectable and the polite and the boring into insurgents—a change very like that undergone by the suicide hijackers of September 11. Those who had previously "lived where motley is worn" suddenly resign their parts "in the casual comedy." The theatrical metaphors suggest that life is a form of art and that violence graduates them to tragedy and a special kind of beauty. He concludes with a celebration of the executed insurrectionists, who will become memorable figures "Wherever green is worn" but only because his writing is memorable, a point insinuated as only Yeats could have done so. Thanks to him, their fame is assured. The art of "Easter, 1916" memorializes the violence which inspired it:

> All changed, changed utterly
> A terrible beauty is born.

In 1983, the avant-garde writer Gordon Lish published *Dear Mr. Capote,* a brilliantly unsettling epistolary novel whose narrator is a serial killer. This man with a knife, who stabs women in the eye, begins by telling Truman Capote, author of *In Cold Blood,* a nonfiction novel about two killers, that he's written this, his first letter, in twelve versions, which he proceeds to produce for Capote's writerly delectation. Like a writer, he's trying out voices because he wants to find the "right one." This is a murderer who is linguistically fastidious in the tradition of Flaubert, a seeker of *le mot just,* but not himself a celebrity novelist and needs one to write his story. The money and the fame—the killer (and Capote) desire them in equal measure—will be good for them both. Lish's novel was published four years after Norman Mailer's *The Executioner's Song,* a nonfictional novel about the killer Gary Gilmore. A fictional murderer and novelist manqué (Lish's antihero) with a yen for an actual novelist (Capote), who was fascinated with actual killers; an actual killer (Gilmore) fascinating an actual novelist (Mailer), who some nineteen years before the publication of *The Executioner's Song* actually knifed his wife. The incestuous relationship between killers and writers is perfectly crystallized. The disturbing adjacency of literary creativity with violence and even political terror is an inheritance of a romantic extremity whose force is still felt. Do killers, artists, and terrorists need one another?

> Dear Mr. Capote, Credit where credit is due. I do not have to suck up to someone in your circle. I myself am in the papers and also on all the channels. I am a household word. . . . All right, I ask you—who has Gotham scared shitless, Norman, me or you?

+ + +

The desire beneath many romantic literary visions is for a terrifying awakening that would undo the West's economic and cultural order, whose origin was the Industrial Revolution and whose goal is global saturation, the obliteration of difference. It is also the desire, of course, of what is called terrorism. Transgressive artistic desire—which wants to make art whose very originality constitutes a step across and beyond the boundaries of the order in place—is desire not to violate within a regime of culture (libel and pornography laws, for example) but desire to stand somehow outside, so much the better to violate and subvert the regime itself.

In the pages ahead, no single, tightly focused "argument" unfolds step by logical step in order to conclude in an incontrovertible generalization, covering all cases, about the nature of transgression in its artistic mode. Nor is this a "history" of transgression, rooted in strategically selected examples, though we think our examples historically provocative indications, each in distinctive ways, of what has been at the core of self-conscious art since the late eighteenth century: an attitude of revolt that defines the way ambitious artists after Kleist routinely conceive of what it means to be an ambitious artist. We offer the reader, instead, extended description and analysis of a web of impulses, expressing themselves in a complex of long and deep running themes, a web that we think catches the unnerving radical spirit of the persistent culture of romanticism. Our intention is to evoke a desperate culture of art, in place today as securely as it was in the literary and political flush times of romantic revolution.

In a series of interwoven and mutually illuminating case studies—moving freely between the realms of high culture and popular culture, fictional and actual people, art and life—various forms of political extremism are related in order to show that to some extent they grow out of avant-garde artistic movements. From romanticism to modernism, these movements consciously presented themselves as revolutionary and sought to shake up—and even overturn—the order of the West. We find that disturbing events of violence and terror—including the events of September 11—are in many ways governed by a logic that grows out of romantic tradition, as life imitates art with a vengeance and real terrorists take their inspiration from books. Transgressive desire again and again on display: encouraging us to reexamine our presuppositions about our artistic heritage and, above all, challenging our easy assumption that art is something always good and at worst benign. But desire for (not an achievement of) an impossible criminality of art eventuates with ruthless fate in failure because cultures inevitably conserve themselves, as they consume and commodify the transgressors.

We assume the familiar theme of transgression and visit it in its violent and artistic forms periodically throughout the book. We sequence the chapters according to an imaginative logic, linking different realms of discourse through thematic dialogues and disturbing juxtapositions of individual works, with reference points tying the chapters together—each reading illuminating the others. This method facilitates our real work: the framing and exploration of our theme's vivid variations—not reducible to one another or to the theme—in a diverse and important group of figures, and actions, not all of them artistic figures or artistic actions in the traditional sense of the word "art." The richness of the idea of "transgressive desire" lies, finally, not in a platonic conception, a theory that explains as it oversees all of the particulars, but in the actual array of aesthetic particulars—those unique and irregular concrete variants that, in themselves and collectively, signify so much more than an abstract concept of transgressive desire. The proof of the pudding lies in the readings, not in the theory, and we shall take it as a compliment, rather than a reprimand, if the reader imagines—as the reader easily will—other readings that we might have made, as relevant as those that we have written.

We may suggest a judgment on our material—and sharpen our theme—by imagining another kind of artistic desire that would seek not to transgress and transform but to pass happily over to the margins, the better to relinquish all ambition for radical social change. To rest with marginality and the understanding that the world will not be altered by artistic acts. To rest with the minimal hope that thanks to the artists, a different way of seeing might be assumed in local pockets of culture, might even make a little change here and there. It is the sort of artistic commitment that doesn't eventuate in failure and despair because such desire is a commitment to permanent exile and renunciation of political ambition. Desire for the margins is at peace with its minority status, even as the secular world abandons and scorns it, leaving it free to create beautiful, challenging things. This is not the aim of the transgressive artist, who wants so much more.

The more clearly we see terror, the less impact we feel from art.

DON DELILLO, *MAO II*

1. GROUNDZEROLAND

It was late in the evening of September 11 and a network special on the day's events was coming to a close. A famous news anchor was saying—these were his final words, solemnly delivered—that tomorrow, when New Yorkers awaken, they will awaken to an altered skyline. Not words about the memory of the dead and the imagination of their terrifying destruction. Nothing to the effect that "our hearts go out" to the ruined families and friends of the dead. Instead, words about a rupture in the perceptual field. A "defamiliarization," as the aesthetic theory of the Russian formalists would have it: that was the deep horror we were left to contemplate by the famous news anchor, who we must not rush to conclude was a shallow, unfeeling man. Let us recall that for most of us—the very greatest majority of us—the thousands slaughtered are abstract. We have no personal connections with them. We never really did, or ever really will, *grieve* for them, though we may think we do so in the world made by Oprah, where human beings assume God's role of feeling everybody's pain.

The famous anchor was in effect predicting that New Yorkers would have an experience of the sort prized by the most advanced imaginative writers and art theorists of the last two centuries. In the perceptual world something new would collapse into view. And tomorrow's newness—awful, to be sure, in more than one sense—would be signified by a hole in the familiar; the absence of two heretofore boring buildings. Those New Yorkers without connection to the dead, the injured, and the displaced would grieve (and fear) not for the dead, the injured, and the displaced but for themselves, undergoing now the terror of the new.

And the rest of us, who do not live in New York? We would like to be invited to make a pilgrimage. We would take our children and our disposable cameras. Acquire the tickets. Then wait in line for as long as it takes to enter and to view. It would please us greatly if Mr. Giuliani, America's mayor, would announce on CNN that we are all welcome to visit Groundzeroland.

+ + +

This much do we learn from Anthony Tommasini, a classical music critic for the *New York Times*, whose provocative report was widely reprinted in American dailies: on September 16, 2001, Karlheinz Stockhausen, the German pioneer of electronic music, and a figure of international renown, was asked at a news conference in Hamburg for his reaction to the terrorist strikes in the United States. He responded by calling the attack on the World Trade Center "the greatest work of art that is possible in the whole cosmos" and went on to speak in apparent awe of the terrorists' achievement of "something in one act" that "we couldn't even dream of in music," in which "people practice like crazy for ten years, totally fanatically for a concert, and then die."

This is our fascination: the transformation of the World Trade Center into a narrative of spectacular images. Terrorism for the camera. (The small section of smoking rubble, that pathetic piece of the Pentagon, a squat and ugly building, holds no appeal.) But Stockhausen is not interested in the images. It is the event itself that entrances him. The event itself is what he means by "the greatest work of art that is possible in the whole cosmos." His incendiary artistic analogy is seriously intended, and he pursues it: "You have people so concentrated on one performance, and then 5,000 people are dispatched into eternity, in a single moment." In the face of such achievement, might Stockhausen be the lesser artist? A touch of envy—envy of terrorism—appears to creep in. "I couldn't do that. In comparison with that, we're nothing as composers."

Stockhausen had been taking questions before the commencement of a four-day festival of his work in Hamburg. His concerts were abruptly canceled; his daughter, a pianist, informed the press that she would no longer appear under the name Stockhausen; international reaction was swift and predictably harsh. In the midst of controversy, he tried to explain: "Where has he brought me, that Lucifer," he asked, referring to a major invented character who regularly figures in a series of seven operas that have engaged him in a twenty-five-year project.

Tommasini acknowledges that Stockhausen "has long been fired by the idea that art should transform us 'out of life itself' . . . otherwise 'it's nothing.' " And Tommasini will allow that "any artwork, from a short Schubert song to a long Dostoevsky novel, can have a transforming effect," but he thinks that a line was crossed. "Stockhausen has dangerously overblown ambitions for art." He's been "losing touch with reality," he's an "egomaniac" and a "raving has-been," who needs to be "confined to a psychiatric clinic."

The extremity of the avant-garde composer's remarks drives the music journalist to a place that the music journalist rarely goes: to theoretical pronouncement. "Art may be hard to define, but whatever it is, it's a step removed from reality." In one breath, Tommasini, a modest man, says that he can't define it; doesn't know what it is; nevertheless will define it; will tell us, in effect, that he knows exactly what it is, when he writes the words "a step removed from reality." He goes on: "A theatrical depiction of suffering may be art; real suffering is not. . . . Images of the blazing twin towers, however horrifically compelling, are not art." (Tommasini, too, is apparently compelled by the blazing towers; the poor Pentagon does not qualify and forget the smoking field of twisted metal in Pennsylvania, because who much talks about that?) Stockhausen's thoughts to the contrary, who was not thinking of the electronic images but of the thing itself, are, for Tommasini, decisive proof of madness. Art is representation ("depiction"); to claim otherwise is not only to announce one's insanity, it is also to impugn what is presumed to be at the core of art: its so-called humanity.

Or perhaps it is to announce, as aesthetic revolutionaries have frequently announced, over the past two centuries, that the war on tradition is a war against what would seem to be the inescapable fact about art—that it is inherently artificial (not life): by definition, "once removed." Aesthetic revolutionaries historically wage polemical war on behalf of the authentic, which they habitually define as an overcoming of precisely traditional art's once-removed character. The famous intention of Wordsworth, for example, to write a language "really spoken" by the rural unprivileged, as opposed to the artificial writing of the poets of his youth, or the intention of his inheritor Robert Frost, by avant-garde standards, like Wordsworth a staid conservative, to "drop to an everyday level of diction that even Wordsworth kept above" and to "entangle," in Frost's words, a living voice in the "syntax, idiom and meaning of a sentence"—these artistic desires of Wordsworth and Frost are alike desires to jump the gap between word and thing (writing and voice) and thereby defeat the mediated or representational character of literature as it has been theorized since Aristotle, who two thousand years before his *New York Times* inheritor argued in the fourth chapter of *The Poetics* that "objects which in themselves we view with pain, we delight to contemplate when reproduced with minute fidelity: such as the forms of the most ignoble animals and"—now an example to the point of September 11—"of dead bodies."

The pain-giving object would appear to be the definitive case for Aristotle, who in his theory of the transformative power of representation argues, in effect, that when an object is relocated from the place in the world where it has its pain-giving being to the realm of an artistic medium, where it is "reproduced" as an image, the pain-giving object becomes pleasurable because we are spared direct interaction with the thing itself. We may merely contemplate it. And our delight lies just there ("we delight to contemplate"), in the contemplative act facilitated by representation, an act presumably made highly unlikely, if not impossible, when we face the real thing in its awful presence.

By the powerful traditional standard set by Aristotle, the pain-giving events themselves of September 11 in New York, as Tommasini argues, are not art. For those on the scene, and their kin and acquaintance, the strike on the towers was only horrific. But the images, on Tommasini's own testimony, are something else. They are "horrifically compelling." In other words, in our contemplative security from the real, the images trigger pleasure—call it engrossed compulsion, the kind of spiritual pleasure attendant on loss of self, as we are absorbed by the transfixing object of our attention. And this very contemplative pleasure, governed by imitation, argues Aristotle, is a deep spring of art. On traditional theoretical grounds, images of ground zero in lower Manhattan may indeed deserve to be called art. How difficult is it to imagine—all that shocking footage artfully edited to become a truly absorbing short film? Absorbing need not entail pleasant. ("And the award for short subjects goes to. . . .")

Does it make any sense to speak, as Stockhausen did, of the aesthetic character and effects of those violently transgressive acts? The events themselves, not their artful representation? To consider the merits of such an idea would require that we put aside the virtually unavoidable sentimentality that asks us to believe that art is always somehow humane and humanizing, that artists, however indecent they might be as human beings, become noble when they make art, which must inevitably ennoble those who experience it.

+ + +

After returning home from his Hamburg debacle, Stockhausen issued this statement on his Web site: "In my work, I have defined Lucifer as the cosmic spirit of rebellion, of anarchy. He uses his high degree of intelligence to destroy creation. . . . I used the designation 'work of art' to mean the work of destruction personified in Lucifer." At the press conference, Stockhausen had been asked if he considered Lucifer's "work of art" to be a criminal act and he answered that it was of course a criminal act because the innocent who were killed had not been given a choice. He added: "But what happened spiritually, this jump out of security, out of the self-evident, out of everyday life [not out of life itself, as Tommasini reports] this sometimes also happens in art . . . or it is worthless." (*Note: also.*) Stockhausen, presciently, asked the assembled journalists not to publish his responses because people "might not understand this."

The Devil, the Arch-Criminal who made Stockhausen speak so scandalously, is not just another character bearing a point of view not necessarily shared by his author but the very figure of artistic ambition (the Arch-Criminal Artist) with which his author identifies. As the mythic destroyer of creation, Lucifer is the destroyer of Somebody Else's creation, Somebody Else's law: "oppressive" is understood as the implied modifier of "creation" and "law." Lucifer, spirit of rebellion and anarchy, has long been the model of the artist, not for Stockhausen alone but for the tradition to which he belongs. *Romantic, prophetic, apocalyptic, revolutionary*—these are the familiar terms used to describe the tradition of the transgressive work of art summed up by Stockhausen as the work of destruction: the destructive power of art that underwrites aesthetic value but is not itself that value. Stockhausen, like Lucifer, is not a nihilist. In Stockhausen's tradition, aesthetic value is the kind of destruction that enables consciousness, or what the Romantic poet Shelley meant when he said that art "strips the film of familiarity" from the world as we know it—the evil of familiarity, a stripping—like an altering of a skyline?—that is a deep cleansing of perception and prelude to the establishment of new consciousness; in Stockhausen's words, an act of imagination with spiritual impact on us—a jump out of security, out of the self-evident, out of everyday life.

Removed from context, Stockhausen's remarks on aesthetic theory are a banality of avant-garde thought. Had he said that the *footage* of the World Trade Center disaster was the greatest work of art possible, his remarks would probably have received only modest attention, to the effect that this is just the kind of thing that this kind of artist is likely to say—an especially insensitive example of *épater le bourgeois.* But Stockhausen referred to the event of mass slaughter and not its filmic reproduction as the greatest work of art, just five days after September 11. His concession that "of course" this was a criminal act because the innocent had no choice—followed hard by his ruthless conjunction ("but what happened spiritually"), seems a pro forma preface to what most excites him: a satanic act that would, *like* an aesthetic act, renovate consciousness through and through.

The terrorists achieved what Stockhausen's kind of artist aspires to. They succeeded in awesome fashion in stripping the film of familiarity from the American view of the world. They seized, they transformed (but for how long?) consciousness. Stockhausen's ambition for his own music, to "break through the routine of time," "to get out of the normal human cycles," in order to "train a new kind of human being," is the cultural ambition of the artist-prophet (a powerful nineteenth-century idea), who viewed himself and his work as a source of truth and justice, and who was to be followed through a cycle of destruction and rebirth; the re-creation of humanity by aesthetic means. In this setting, the terrorist events of September 11 are isomorphic with Stockhausen's aesthetic theory, and it is not difficult to understand why he would be swept away, as an artist, by them.

+ + +

Three discriminations:

1. As any avant-garde artist might, Stockhausen sees the devotion of high artistic seriousness (like Flaubert, like Joyce) in the complete commitment of the terrorists, which he likens to practicing "like crazy for ten years, totally fanatically for a concert." Like terrorists, serious artists are always fanatics; unlike terrorists, serious artists have not yet achieved the "greatest" level of art. Note: "greatest" is not a claim for uniqueness but a claim for the terrorists' continuity with what serious artists in Stockhausen's tradition always try for: "great," "greater," "greatest" signify ascending degrees of influencing mass consciousness; at the superlative stage of art, and terror, consciousness is not merely influenced: it is transformed.
2. As for that key word, *transformation:* Stockhausen's madness, according to Tommasini, who will not mind standing here for the reasonable point of view, lies in his taking of transformative possibilities in art at face value—transformation not, in Aris-

totelian fashion, of the object, in order to provide a congenial occasion for contemplative reflection and pleasure, an occasion for cognition unimpeded by emotion, but transformation of the attending consciousness itself, an occasion for the emergence of a New Man and a New World. And transformation is not qualifiable. There cannot be, as Tommasini seems to want, a small, safe transformation, with the majority of consciousness (and world) untouched and secure in all the old familiar places. Transformation is either total (and revolutionary) or it is not transformation; failure of transformation is failure of art and terror. In true transformation, we are possessed and catapulted out of the ordinary—taken over by original vision with no wiggle room for rational escape. Such aesthetic experience may be apocalyptically political, or it may be the sort of experience pointed to in Tommasini's reference to a "short Schubert song": an experience of ravishment (interior apocalypse), which for its modest duration takes us away and renders us useless for the affairs of everyday life.

3. When Stockhausen slips and says that what happened in New York on September 11 "also" may happen in art, or art is worthless, he tells us that his intentions as an artist are as ambitious as those of the terrorists, that he wants art to have that kind of force. In this way would he be a terrorist of art. The terrorists did the thing that he would do but hasn't yet done, having not yet reached in his music the plateau of "the greatest." And he tells us clearly, but perhaps not yet himself, still swept up as he is by the seductive idea of September 11, that the event at the World Trade Center is not art. Stockhausen's logical slippage, marked by his "also," is just this: his idea of art is a subset of the category of transgression; the category includes many acts—criminal and punishable by law, as Stockhausen's music is not—that are not art. Which is to say: transgression and its desired effect, transformation, are not uniquely artistic phenomena. Stockhausen's transcendental ambition to transgress and transform is only the latest indicator of what ambitious artists

> have most feared for the past two centuries—their cultural inconsequence, looming now more than ever, in the Age of Television.

No one has yet seriously proposed that Stockhausen, for having composed what he's composed, should be incarcerated. Tommasini does urge incarceration, but that in a clinic for the insane—incarceration deserved not for what Stockhausen composed but for what he proposed in his theory of great art.

+ + +

"Getting shot is for real . . . there's no element of pretence or make-believe in it": Chris Burden, the performance artist, speaking of *Shoot* (1971). A real-time activity (an actual shooting); a body subjected to risk and serious pain (Burden's); a violent act whose goal, nevertheless, is to trigger "mental stuff," says Burden, in those who take it in. Illusion is false. Here is total disdain for the mainstream West's Aristotelian theater of representation. Though of course an audience is desired: that's the contradiction. This is not antitheater after all. Something is to be done to those who take it in. A wish to communicate not *about* the real but to communicate the real itself, thrust it bodily through the space separating performer and viewer. Performance art is ontological-didactic theater.

Or consider the big event—site-specific, environmental. An elaborate spectacle requiring advanced technology. A theater of images, set in an unconventional location, requiring a huge cast and crew and, in its audience, competence in visual grammar: a theater on behalf of perception—not text or story. Robert Wilson says, "Listen to images." Performance art in the 1990s was art more and more with an agenda. A theater of lessons, visually encoded.

In spite of their *intentions*, which not even Stockhausen called aesthetic, the suicide terrorists who struck New York may be said to have made—with the cooperation of American television—performance art with political designs on its American audience. The site, the World Trade Center, was unconventional and politically loaded: the symbolic center of globalized capitalism. Advanced technology was mastered and put into play. The cast was huge; bodies were subjected to serious pain. All of this in real time, with no element of pretense or make-believe in it. Thanks to the cameras, which bin Laden could confidently assume would be there, images of a spectacular sort were generated, framed, and replayed endlessly. Thanks to the presence of the camera, which guaranteed a vast audience, this act of performance *means* something, achieves the paradoxical fusion of "life" and "art," "event" and its filmic representation in minute and faithful reproduction.

In more traditional terms: there were authors (bin Laden, Atta, etc.); there was plot—a structure of events with deep narrative inevitability; there were thousands of characters—but with no choice in turning down the role, with no knowledge that they'd been cast to die. And there was an audience with no choice but to experience terrorist narrative once that narrative found its true medium of communication, the media without which terrorist art is ineffective and which complicitously completes its totalitarian trajectory: to saturate consciousness in the United States with the thought of terror, with no sanctuary left for the blessed banalities of ordinary life. They would make Americans forever insecure; cause us to join the rest of the world, at last; and end, at last, our long holiday from history. They would change us.

And the mainspring of this aesthetic experience is an absence, a rubble pit in lower Manhattan—that rupture in the perceptual field which marks the original art of the suicide pilots.

+ + +

When Gottfried Semper designed the Bayreuth Festival Playhouse, which opened in 1876, he placed the audience on one single "classless" level, a feature anticipated by Wagner himself (the director of the design) in keeping with his anticommercial, antibourgeois, pro-"folk" theoretical stance. Semper would build community by leveling the tiers of the traditional theater, erasing class difference, and creating a "mystic gulf" between the audience and the stage. On December 30, 2001, Mayor Giuliani opened a viewing platform for the folk over the mystic gulf that is Ground Zero, a stage to which he urged Americans, and everybody, to come and experience "all kinds of feelings of sorrow and then tremendous feelings of patriotism." Though concerned that some would come for "the wrong reasons," whatever they might be, he was sure most would go for "the right reasons," whatever those are. "Tourist attraction" or "hallowed ground"? Or "tourist attraction" and "hallowed ground"? Heavily supported by the New York tourist and convention bureau, the platform proposal "glided through unusually dense thickets of red tape." Restaurants and hotel beds had been empty too long.

Herbert Muschamp of the *New York Times* articulates what sounds like a manifesto of an artistic movement with a political agenda in his description of the design of the platform: "The design does hold meaning. It embodies stoic principles. It treats the need for design as a reduction to essentials. The result has substance. Stop the mystification, the grandiosity, the use of architecture to disconnect our history from ourselves. Give the city back." Give us back our exceptionalism. Because the long American holiday from history is far from over.

The platform's purpose is to connect tourists to their history at a site that perfectly conjoins terrorism, patriotism, and tourism. A ticket is available, as yet for no charge, for those cold, sad pilgrims who would like to connect to their history, without mediation and with maximum transparency, without waiting in line: a ticket stamped for a specific time, for a specific fifteen-minute interval. Andy Warhol's whisper echoes in the time limit on the platform, that magic fifteen minutes, the promise of future fame for everybody: the leveling of class difference. FastPass to Magic Mountain. FastPass to Groundzeroland.

People don't know what they're looking at. The platform will tell them. Pictures are snapped; souvenir hats and pretzels are bought; T-shirts are sold; designer sunglasses are hawked. The first fortunate pilgrim gets his name in the paper just as he did when he snagged first place in line for the World Series. Tourists come from Japan to see "this reality," what one grieving mother described as "my child's body all over that place." Collectors or curators "relying on aesthetic judgment," randomly but not accidentally, select objects to be stored for future exhibition. They call them "*art*ifacts," artifacts of terror, and by virtue of their selection and acquisition, the city of New York in effect lends credibility to

Stockhausen's perception of the terrorist attack as "the greatest work of art that is possible in the whole cosmos." The madman approaches vindication.

The only problem is how can the traces of her child's body all over the place be removed from the artifacts without destroying them. In some cultures, the curators would be perceived as vultures engaged in an act of desecration, an act of grave robbing. The value of an object selected by curators immediately becomes "incalculable," whereas unselected objects end up in the junkyard, without value, or sold for recycling—lacking the "power to stir the imaginations and the souls of visitors." One firefighter, outraged at first at a curator taking digital photographs of the gravesite of his brothers, was soon transformed into a curator himself with the understanding of "an archive, a memorial," destined perhaps for the Smithsonian, so that others will understand.

The tourists think their presence is a gift to the grieving. One man's grief is another man's right to reality. Surrounding offices into which determined tourists try to break, enforcing their right to see, are choice skyboxes to the towerless void, this "fake New York." Seeing the pit on television, seeing the representation, does not provide sufficient meaning. The pilgrimage must be made to the so much bigger, so much more surreal Groundzeroland. They claim their right to look. Democracy gives them the right to look, to take back the view that was stolen from them.

In his novel, *The Sheltering Sky*, Paul Bowles draws a sharp distinction between tourists, deserving of scorn, who journey for a fixed period of time, and travelers, brave adventurers who might never return. Travelers might find true reality in Evan Fairbanks's twenty-five-minute video of the attack—history playing at the New York Historical Society—the only mediation that of the documentarian's soundless camera. Where is the grassy knoll—on TV, in the pit, or in the mind?

If George Bush is right that we should show patriotism by going on vacation and spending money, then visiting Groundzeroland is a patriotic act. The sublime power of American consumer culture to absorb and commodify even such a devastating blow as this transgressive act of destruction and murder is final proof of that culture's fundamental indestructibility. Walk up the ramp to the platform without filter and, for a golden fifteen minutes, see the erasure—see what isn't there—and see what cannot be erased: the meeting ground for the producers and consumers of popular culture. Experience the Warholian conflation of violent, tragic, mass media news with the patriotic glory and glamour of death. Pose for a picture: mix disaster and death with stardom and beauty. Feel the scale. Absorb it. Go down in history. Move on. Understand it all. Find closure.

2. LITERARY TERRORISTS

From Wordsworth to Don DeLillo, the intention of the "serious artist," as Ezra Pound called him, is consistent: to alter consciousness, shape and influence the "inner life of the culture," in DeLillo's words, for the ultimate purpose of shaping and influencing the culture's outer life, the social design itself. Since about 1800, the serious artist is the would-be criminal violator of the order of things, and his role remains consistently romantic because the social condition, for all of its vast changes since Wordsworth, remains, according to serious artists, in deep structural ways, what it was in Wordsworth's day.

What defense does Wordsworth offer for becoming an enemy of the people? The classic apologia of the avant-garde artist: that he is in reality the people's good doctor. A defense on the way to the highly educated, manifesto-writing American murderer who was likened in the pages of the *New Yorker*, by Cynthia Ozick, to Dostoevsky's antihero of *Crime and Punishment:* the domestic terrorist known as the Unabomber, Theodore Kaczynski, whom Ozick describes as a "philosophical criminal" of "humanitarian purpose." Wordsworth's defense is that the people are sick unto death and require the medicine of his life-giving literary violence. They are unfit for "all voluntary exertion"—they are not free. They have been reduced, in their condition of unfreedom, "to a state of almost savage torpor," and chief among the causes, says Wordsworth, agrees Kaczynski, is what we call modernization—"the accumulation of men in cities" and the "uniformity of their occupations," which convert them, these makers of products, in Kaczynski's extension of Wordsworth, into replicants, "engineered products" themselves. These causes constitute, says Wordsworth, agrees Kaczynski, "a general evil." And the causes of this "general evil" have themselves a famous prime cause: the Industrial Revolution, which, again like Kaczynski, Wordsworth believes to have been (in Kaczynski's words) a "disaster for the human race." The time is approaching, he says with apocalyptic implication, "when the evil will be systematically opposed, by men of greater powers, and with far more distinguished success." By "greater powers" Wordsworth seems to mean more-than-literary power; he apparently refers to men of ruthless force, as he recollects the great passion of his young manhood: the French Revolution. Systematic opposition suggests attack on the system itself, in its material form: not literary explosives but actual explosives.

With the stakes so high, the writer must take extreme measures. He must build cultural bombs:

> It is supposed, that by the act of writing in verse an Author makes a formal engagement that he will gratify certain known habits of association . . . but it will undoubtedly appear to many persons that I have not fulfilled the terms of an engagement thus voluntarily contracted . . . they will look around for poetry, and will be induced to inquire by what species of courtesy these attempts can be permitted to assume that title.

Thus Wordsworth, near the beginning of his preface to the second edition of *Lyrical Ballads* (1800), the founding critical document of a revolutionary literary movement in English literature. He feels himself step outside the mainstream of literary history, wherein writers—and their theorist-apologists since Plato—tend to conceive of themselves as quintessential insiders, cultural enforcers, comfortably contracted: artistic conservers of the standing culture's ideology—its values and the story that it likes to tell about itself—precisely unlike Wordsworth the destroyer, the would-be instigator of radical change, literary and social, who would break with the culture in place and bear adversarial values and vision. Literary change, in this perspective, is a step toward social change and the restoration of our humanity—social change as social reversal. Serious artists since Wordsworth often cultivate a critical nostalgia.

Wordsworth worries (uneasy rebel) that he has broken the contract that all writers voluntarily sign when they set before the public a book of "poems." Readers in 1800, who'd cut their teeth on Shakespeare, Donne, Herbert, and Milton, on Pope and Thomas Gray, could not but feel their literary sensibilities assaulted and battered by this outrageous prosaic flatness from Wordsworth, offered as "poetry."

> I saw an aged Beggar in my walk,
> And he was seated by the highway side
> On a low structure of rude masonry
> Built at the foot of a huge hill . . .

Wordsworth believes that he will rightly be seen to have subverted the publicly contracted expectations of his day and violated the "formal engagement" that historically has bound writer and reading public. He tells us that the contract changes from era to era but that there must always be one. Violation of contract is a crime, committed here by Wordsworth with premeditation, as an act of cultural first-degree murder, the assassination of the current idea of poetry—a deed of literary terrorism on behalf of an originality that, by definition, cannot be contracted, defined, or publicly known in advance of its disruptive appearance.

It is therefore the author's desire for originality—for unknown points of association—that causes breach of contract. By refusing to gratify, per contract, known habits of association, the author refuses to repeat what has been written, even by himself. And this refusal to perform the duty imposed on him by literary tradition bespeaks not "indolence," says Wordsworth, but a desire to free himself from enslavement to the past. What late capitalism will come to crave in cultural production, as obviously in industrial production, is precisely the manipulation of artists into mindless mechanisms of repetition, effectively producing standardized artworks: "commodity" or "product," the sign of the general suppression of all idiosyncratic impulse. What the transgressive artist relentlessly desires, on the other hand, is the insistent recarving out of all outlines of personality and all human variety. The transgressive artist, then, in active rebellion against the culture's need to commodify him, creates "something living, something capable of constant transformation"—Pound's definition of the character of serious literature. The crime of the authentic artist is nothing other than the crime of originality.

We are sick, and shall become sicker. Our "savage torpor" produces a craving for "extraordinary incident, which the rapid communication of intelligence hourly gratifies." Craving for stimulation of the "gross and violent" sort stems, it is thought, Wordsworth to the Unabomber, from the impact of an industrial system of production, the technology of which, in its side effects, converts the operators of machines into machines themselves, or "cogs in the social machine," in Kaczynski's importantly hackneyed words—laborers whose repetitious acts make them over into repetitions of one another and rob them in one stroke of their "individuality" and their "freedom" (terms interchangeable, Wordsworth to DeLillo to Kaczynski). We crave catastrophe as the antidote to "savage torpor," and the news media in 1800, such as it was, already ministers to that lurid craving:

> We're giving way to terror, to news of terror, to tape recorders and cameras, to radios, to bombs stashed in radios. News of disaster is the only narrative people need. The darker the news, the grander the narrative. News is the last addiction. . . .

That is the DeLillo of 1991, via the hero of *Mao II,* toward whom, in 1800, Wordsworth was making his way.

Against his vision of modern hell—technologically undergirded and situated in England's emerging wasteland of smoky cities—Wordsworth poises his organic counterideal. In describing the "humble and rustic" subject of his poems, he gives us this rationale for choosing that subject: "because the manners of rural life germinate from . . . elementary feelings, and, from the necessary character of rural occupations." Those "elementary feelings" or "essential passions" are, moreover, "incorporated"—they find their true body in the "beautiful and permanent forms of nature." In the rural world, human behavior "germinates" like a plant whose matrix (in Kaczynski's phrase) is "wild nature." Wordsworth, like Kaczynski, thought rural existence hard—hard but rooted in necessary (natural) reality, as life in the metropolis (T. S. Eliot's "Unreal City") was not. Wordsworth and Kaczynski are transgressive philosophers of the pastoral—one of imaginative acts, almost always free from the law, the other of bloody deeds, now incarcerated for life.

From the traditional (and reasonable) literary point of view, Wordsworth's preface is outlandishly arrogant—the paradigm of criminal artistic intention, announced by a writer who tells us that the world created by the new technology is "evil"—note: a theological term—and that he, ostensibly sane, would redeem it by writing lyric poems in a new manner, that in order to succeed he must violate the popular culture of the day—"frantic novels, sickly and stupid German Tragedies, and deluges of idle and extravagant stories in verse"—because this culture and its news media feeds and reproduces the "general evil." Popular culture, a "deluge," swamps consciousness—Wordsworth's metaphor resonates through the Unabomber and DeLillo (who writes of a "blur and glut"); so swamped we become usefully torpid citizens of the order of things. The transgressive artist believes himself to be the one undegraded opponent of a corpsed world—weaponless except for the originality of his writing: the only humane countercultural response, whose failure would necessitate physical force.

+ + +

Never forget that the human race with technology is just like an alcoholic with a barrel of wine.

THE UNABOMBER

When Bill Gray, the writer-hero of DeLillo's *Mao II,* was a boy, he used to announce ballgames to himself. It was harmless play, free of cultural ambition: he calls it the "lost game of self, without fear or doubt." "I was

the players, the announcer, the crowd, the listening audience and the radio. . . . And I've been trying to write toward that kind of innocence ever since. The pure game of making up." In this suspended game—self-sufficient, spontaneous, seamless—imagination, as the presiding deity of subjective space, would stand in opposition to terrorism. Now, however, no more "pure game." When he grows up to become a novelist, Bill grows a not so innocent desire for cultural power. Now, he thinks, "there's no longer a moral or spatial distinction between thinking and acting," and terror is the logical endpoint of his literary ambition for cultural impact, the zone where thinking and acting collide in the public world with the force of an explosion:

> To make an impression on society with words is . . . almost impossible for most individuals and small groups. Take us for example. If we had never done anything violent and had submitted the present writings to a publisher, they probably would not have been accepted. If they had been accepted and published, they probably would not have attracted many readers, because it's more fun to watch the entertainment put out by the media than to read a sober essay. . . . In order to get our message before the public with some chance of making a lasting impression, we've had to kill people.

Thus the man known as the Unabomber, Theodore John Kaczynski, who tells us that what he desired was not to kill people but "to make an impression on society with words," surely irrefutable evidence of Kaczynski's total madness. The Unabomber would have preferred (like Bill Gray or Wordsworth) to initiate radical change with his writing. He came quickly to understand (like Bill Gray) that violent acts are now necessary if the "inner life of the culture" is to be seriously affected. Once its attention has been commanded by his violence, the culture might be ready to read him seriously, and in large numbers, and then, and only then, under his writerly persuasion, sweep away the advanced technological conditions of production. Kaczynski is a "literary" man in an older sense: a man of words, with educative designs on his society, who would influence the shape of things to come. The surest way, in Unabomber logic, of recapturing the serious artist's ideal of the writer as a culture-shaping

force is to do spectacular serial murder, for the purpose of becoming America's most famous terrorist within. As a media star, however dark, publishers would be eager to take him on, and they did, though under heavy humanitarian cover. The *New York Times* and the *Washington Post* published his small book, *Industrial Society and Its Future* (1995), they said, in the hope of saving lives.

Kaczynski's intention—derisively (and imprecisely) called, by the media's talking heads, Luddite—was to reverse the technological clock and put in the place of industrial society technology's eternal counterideal, wild nature, "those aspects of the functioning of the earth," as he writes, "and its living things that are independent of human management and free of human interference and control." He means, as his *Manifesto* makes clear in several places, that if we can only undo technology we'll revive the living things, especially of the human type, that have long been interfered with in our enlightened quest to rationalize and control nature for the betterment of human life.

Kaczynski's *Manifesto*, and the literary line opened by Mary Shelley's *Frankenstein* (1818) and culminating in DeLillo's *White Noise* (1985), stand four-square against the enlightened mind: against modernity. The common mistake of not distinguishing Dr. Viktor Frankenstein from the monster he creates—the monster is often called Frankenstein—yields an insight. What is the monster if not the embodiment of a will unable to control the consequences of its acts for the good of mankind, the violent unintended side effect that undoes Dr. Frankenstein's conscious intention: to defeat death itself.

In the closing scene of Mary Shelley's prophetic novel, the monster delivers a monologue in which he tells us that he intends to commit suicide: "I shall collect my funeral pile and consume to ashes this miserable frame." Which is the way that the most recent film version by Kenneth Branagh concludes, with the monster ablaze at the Arctic Circle, in his funeral pile, but not the way the novel ends. Shelley chose not to write that theatrically satisfying scene and instead wrote this final sentence: "He sprang from the cabin window as he said this, upon the ice raft which lay close to the vessel. He was soon borne away by the waves and lost in darkness and distance." Whatever she intended by her final scene, Mary Shel-

ley's closing words permit another, more sinister interpretation, one that DeLillo, Kaczynski, and other connoisseurs of the technological side effect could appreciate. The monster does not die, he just disappears. As the figure of death overcome, how could he die, even though he has a desire to do so, and would act on that desire? The monster, the unintended side effect, is at large and insidiously active. Let us call this implication of Shelley's close "the Frankenstein effect," in order to describe how the enlightened will's good intentions result in unwanted consequences of malevolent and irretrievable impact. Those toxic spills are not what we meant, not at all, and Dr. Frankenstein is ourselves.

Kaczynski's plan "to overthrow the economic and technological basis of the present society" is no expression of a radical environmentalist because his counterideal of wild nature is not, finally, about protecting the green world but about winning back for human beings the freedom that technology has taken from them. What technology robs us of, he writes, is our "autonomy" (a cherished key word) and therefore the basis of our well-being. We are ill, he argues, because we are nothing but "engineered products" of the technological system that structures our relations to the world. Unlike actual commodities, the pure human products of modernity go crazy as they suffer (in Kaczynski's words) "boredom, demoralization, low self-esteem, inferiority feelings, defeatism, depression, anxiety, guilt, frustration, hostility, spouse or child abuse, insatiable hedonism, abnormal sexual behavior, sleep disorders, eating disorders, etc." The arguments and observations of Kaczynski, who was much portrayed as a freak and madman, are reiterations of major themes in continental philosophy running from the German idealists to the Frankfurt School, and in the literary tradition from Wordsworth to the modernists to Pynchon and DeLillo. Kaczynski's banality and so-called madness are representative.

Of course, every technological advance is put into operation, he acknowledges, because it provides an obvious benefit: Technology, and its technicians, like Dr. Frankenstein, have only (in the main) good intentions. So we are not pushed by evil will, but we drift, slowly but steadily into ever greater dependency on various advances until we become puppets of the technological system as a whole. The intention is good, the ultimate effect, totalitarian. Like the monster of Mary Shelley's novel, the system assumes a life and will of its own beyond the control of human reason, whose creature it is.

> If the machines are permitted to make all their own decisions, we can't make any conjectures as to the results, because it is impossible to guess how such machines might behave. We only point out that the fate of the human race would be at the mercy of the machines. . . . We are suggesting neither that the human race would voluntarily turn power over to the machines nor that the machines would willfully seize power. What we do suggest is that the human race might easily permit itself to drift into a position of such dependence on the machines that it would have no practical choice but to accept all of the machines' decisions. . . . Eventually a stage may be reached at which the decisions necessary to keep this system running will be so complex that human beings will be incapable of making them intelligently. At that stage machines will be in effective control. People won't be able to just turn the machines off, because they will be so dependent on them that turning them off would amount to suicide.

In the face of this more-than-imminent neo-Orwellian apocalypse, what is to be done? If we are nothing but a mass of replications, "engineered products," as Kaczynski says, "flooded" by the mass media's entertainment and its endless glut of "gross and violent" images—he has in mind the electronic form of Valium, the world of television—how are we to emerge from our torpidity? How to make a new start? He says: by an answering act of original violence. Original as pertaining to an origin, originating a new beginning. First, acts of hard-core criminality, a series of bombings. Followed by an act of soft-core criminality, the publication of his philosophical essay. Then the revolution. And at the end of it all, the possibility of life lived harmoniously in small organic communities (as Wordsworth hoped), nature dependent. *Autonomy* is a key term for Kaczynski, but *community* is the greater key because it is in community, paradoxically, that autonomy is nourished and preserved.

Theodore Kaczynski may be, as Cynthia Ozick writes in the *New*

Yorker, "America's own Raskolnikov," the "visionary murderer" of Dostoevsky's *Crime and Punishment.* But maybe not. A man of exceptional intelligence, certainly. And moreover possessed (in more ways than one) by "humanitarian purpose," as Ozick writes. What, though, are we to make of the appalling, flat tone of this humanitarian: "In order to get our message before the public with some chance of making a lasting impression, we've had to kill people." Philosopher-criminal, or just criminal, psychotic killer of no affect sending bombs to scientists, from the wilds of Montana, under cover of what Ozick thinks "uncompromising idealism"?

Kill strangers, on purpose, on behalf of an idea (for a better world).

Kill all the Dr. Frankensteins before they make more monsters.

+ + +

> Surrealism was not afraid to make for itself a tenet of total revolt, complete insubordination, of sabotage according to rule, and . . . it . . . expects nothing save from violence. The simplest Surrealist act consists of dashing down into the street, pistol in hand, and firing blindly, as fast as you can pull the trigger, into the crowd. Anyone who, at least once in his life, has not dreamed of thus putting an end to the petty system of debasement and cretinization in effect has a well-defined place in that crowd, with his belly at barrel level.
>
> ***SECOND MANIFESTO OF SURREALISM***

Joseph Cornell, the surrealist artist, created boxes that made the art of assemblage into a true poetic form, a blast of illumination. A literal bomb explosion in the manner of Kaczynski, a serious artist and himself a maker of boxes, is the extremity of James Joyce's idea of an epiphany, the gentler form of shaping a consciousness. Cornell's boxes were Jewel Cases, Museums, Pharmacies, Aviaries (some with blood-spattered birds), and Habitats, designed to evoke the games and toys of childhood, Victorian parlors, and other things past—puzzles, messages. By varnishing and polishing wood, he made it look antique. He collaged pages from old books on the backs of his boxes to create the appearance of age. He left boxes to the elements for weathering and even subjected one to an oven's heat to peel and crack the inner paint—to send it deeper into the past.

Theodore Kaczynski spent most of his adult life inside a 10′ by 12′ cabin, his very existence a Cornellian box. As a boy, he crafted beautiful, intricate objects, like a sewing box for the thirteen-year-old daughter of a family friend. As a budding mathematical genius at Evergreen Park High School in Illinois, he sent to Joann Vincent De Young, a young girl with whom he was infatuated, a little wad of paper that exploded when she opened it—a testament to his erotic feeling for her. Later, he combined, in the surrealist mode of association, the making of boxes—he had a connoisseur's interest in various woods—with the making of bombs. In one of his earliest acts, he hid a bomb within the pages of a novel called *Ice Brothers.* Surrounded in his cabin-box by stacks of Shakespeare, Thackeray, Victor Hugo, and Conrad, Kaczynski fashioned his own surrealist agenda. Scraping labels off batteries, using stamps issued long ago, wires out of production (all old objects in the service of recollecting his childhood games: blowing up weeds, creating an explosion in a garbage can, setting off a rocket, making little popping devices called Atomic Pearls), he made works of art that killed people. He sanded the bombs down to remove fingerprints and oils from the hands that crafted them. His artifacts were untraceable. Craft, nostalgia, isolation—the triple vocation of serious artists, Kaczynski and Cornell.

Many of Cornell's boxes were guides to astronomy, science, and mathematics. His first box, one of many artistic puzzles, contained elements that would repeat throughout his career: a circular map, a clay pipe, a cordial glass, a doll's head, an egg. Kaczynski's art-box bombs also contained repeating elements—his artistic signature, as it were. Kaczynski, the artisan, deployed the ordinary objects "really used by men"—furniture pieces, plumbing pipes, sink traps—and hand-, not machine-, made screws and triggers. Wordsworth deployed "the language really used by men"—as opposed to the language found only in books of poetry—"with a certain colouring of imagination thrown over" it, to fashion cultural bombs. In creating explosives from common objects, Kaczynski likewise throws "a certain colouring of imagination" over them. Following his literary-theoretical predecessor, Kaczynski desires that the passions of men be "incorporated with the beautiful and permanent forms of nature." He did not use plastic. He did not use Semtex H.

This briefcase boy with the pocket protector, this brilliant mathematician, tried to evoke a world that no longer exists and, in the process, created a legend—*un* for university, plus *a* for airline, plus *bomber*—the Unabomber, pictured wearing the hooded sweatshirt of the terrorist. The imagination of Theodore Kaczynski flies to a utopian world at last inhabitable. André Breton would consider him "blessed with violence," but what would Breton's answer be to this question: Does violence, in the person of Kaczynski, compromise or not?

+ + +

DeLillo's writer-hero, Bill Gray, speaks with longing, as he thinks back on the role of the artist in society:

> There's a curious knot that binds novelists and terrorists. In the West we become famous effigies as our books lose power to shape and influence. . . . Years ago I used to think it was possible for a novelist to alter the inner life of the culture. Now bomb-makers and gunmen have taken that territory. They make raids on human consciousness. What writers used to do before we were all incorporated.

The alternative ("altering") vision of the novelist, a would-be raider of consciousness, once reshaped our thoughts and feelings about the world in place—the world that the transgressive artist would violate in order to remake. But no more. In the advanced technological culture of the United States, the writer is rendered impotent by virtue of his being consumed by the image factories of electronic capitalism, whose most duplicitous agent is commercial publishing, which would make the writer a "famous effigy." "The secret force that drives the industry," writes DeLillo, "is the compulsion to make writers harmless." Bill Gray believes—ten years before September 11—that our new tragic narrative "involves midair explosions and crumbled buildings." It is the terrorist, "the lethal believer, the person who kills and dies for faith," who shapes the way we think and see: it is the terrorist that we in the West take seriously, not the celebrity-writer, who has been appropriated by the culture of capital.

In a culture so addicted to the image, vampirish fame feeds at the throat of the writer, whose work, with shocking ease, is now wholly sucked into his image, the name and the face: tomb of his would-be adversarial writing. Consider Bill Gray, whose disappearance more than twenty years ago has only served to spike the sales of his earlier books and make them modern classics, and him famous. Even the writer's refusal to allow his picture to be taken becomes, against his will, his ticket to fame, big sales, and social irrelevance: Thomas Pynchon. The absent image becomes his image: J. D. Salinger. The book itself, which used to represent the transgressive novelist's desire to do harm to the familiar, change consciousness, and thereby the social design, gives way to this final superficiality: the author's circulating photograph (or desire for the withheld photo), the be-all and end-all of celebrity and the displacement—by a glittering surface—of an art that has traditionally made claim to substance, to depth.

Knowing that he cannot win the image game, and after all those years in hiding, Bill commits his image to film—a gesture he believes to be the announcement of his dying, death precipitated by the fear that he's lost his talent. His subsequent decision to offer up his body, to trade places with his double, an obscure Swiss poet held hostage in Lebanon, is therefore both a political and literary act, the last, desperate means available to him to reenter the stream of the inner life of his culture and become what his culture needs in order to see itself clearly, in its dehumanized state, so much the better to change itself.

Mao II is a novel of ideas, and at its heart lies the argument that novelists and terrorists play a zero-sum game. In Bill's words: "What terrorists gain, novelists lose. The degree to which they influence mass consciousness is the extent of our decline as shapers of sensibility and thought. The danger they represent equals our failure to be dangerous." What Wordsworth thought a new literary role—the writer as contract buster—and what he must therefore offer a defense for—some two hundred years later is taken as a given of the serious artistic life: that the writer's function is to influence and shape sensibility and thought and that such an act is, or should be, a "dangerous" act, because by "influence" and "shape" Wordsworth, DeLillo, and Company really mean "change at the root." Should be a dangerous act, but is no more; Bill is nostalgic.

A spokesman for a terrorist group tells Bill that in a society reduced to "blur and glut"—the "rush of endless streaming images," messages poured from the media and repeated and repeated—in such a context our consciousness sinks into passivity, becomes itself a TV set running ads and news, the same ads, the same news. All is assimilated: madmen, thugs, and artists alike, "absorbed and processed and incorporated"—reduced to "savage torpor," electronically induced (Wordsworth's phrase is more relevant than ever). Only the terrorist breaks through, because he alone secretly excites us, because the culture has not "figured out how to assimilate him." Bill agrees with the Wordsworthian diagnosis but rejects the medicine of terror. The terrorist, he replies, is no "solitary outlaw"—a description he'd like to (but can't) reserve for himself; he's an instrument of repressive governments, a "perfect little totalitarian state" seeking to impose "total order" via "total destruction."

The counterideal to fascism and actual bloodletting violence is suggested by Bill's moving description of his creative process as a would-be antithesis to the world of repetitions and human automatons: "The experience of my own consciousness tells me how autocracy fails, how total control wrecks the spirit, how my characters deny my efforts to own them completely, how I need internal dissent, self-argument, how the world squashes me the minute I think it's mine." The process of writing the novel provides him with his principle of freedom, grounded not in politics per se but in the dynamic of creation. In its unfolding, writing becomes the site of freedom's emergence, the image of freedom's victory for the individual over the totalitarian principle, identified here not with some exterior figure of fascism but as the totalitarian within us all, radically democratic novelist included, who wants to, he confesses, but finally cannot—in this nod to Pirandello—own and control his characters. "Characters," in this sense, are representations of the finally uncontrollable, the free self. So the writer is a democratic champion in spite of himself, champion of a self that escapes his desire to dominate, and that self is none other than the writer's own insubordinate artistic consciousness, in disagreement with himself, the one thing in the world not subject to the totalitarian urge, the one indomitable thing that Bill knows: aesthetic last refuge of the truly human. It is a bleak and perhaps finally self-serving theory of art that Bill entertains, one that in the whole of *Mao II* DeLillo will resist, and in so resisting put himself at odds with the aesthetic humanism of the romantic and modernist literary traditions and their generally secular and liberal alternatives to the modernized world—alternatives that significant writers in those traditions have, nevertheless, vigorously despised.

DeLillo presents the image, the novelist, and the terrorist as a contemporary cultural intersection, in the hope of troubling the great postmodern complacency, the dogma of the image that would supplant the real. Beneath the image, so it goes in the ideology of postmodernism, no foundational uniqueness of self or art that provides the basis for repetition of the image. In the beginning, says postmodernism, no beginning, no First Thing, no origin. Rather, in the beginning, there is repetition—the motor, as it were, of advanced commodity culture. That part of DeLillo that sympathizes with his hero writes *Mao II* in an effort to influence (*influence* with kinship to *influenza*), in order to infect with the disease that would cure, that fortunate disease signified by the key value terms, political and literary, since Romanticism and the late eighteenth century and the rise of democracy. *Originality, creativity, individuality,* and *freedom* are synonymous terms in modern Western culture and, together, they comprise the index of an authentic selfhood that is the matrix of a unique literary style. The artist is rigorous champion and superb representative of the unique, free self, and his culture is its rigorous and superb denier, marginalizer, destroyer.

In the culture of the engineered commodity (infinitely replicated products, human and otherwise) now hideously reinforced and replayed in the electronic society of the image, the prized value is not originality: Campbell soup cans, Coke bottles, pictures of Mao and Marilyn—so much the better to consume our Campbell's, our Coke, our Mao, and our Marilyn. Human product consuming product. Are they so different, our Mao and our Marilyn? Are they not both dead and famous? Andy Warhol becomes the ambivalent god of this culture (parodist? cynical sustainer?), and therefore the discomforting genius of DeLillo's novel and, more, the discomforting *genius loci* of the contemporary West. The desire for originality in writing and in selfhood, for that which cannot be repeated without being destroyed, is a desire triggered by a culture of numbing sameness, in the disguise of democracy. What is wanted, in the words of Wallace Stevens, who would have understood DeLillo, is the "quick" and the "unaccountable," our only means of escape from all manner of police (economic, literary, electronic) and their prison houses of repetition.

The terrorist Abu Rashid, who holds the Swiss poet and covets the famous Bill Gray, replicates his own image on his child and the boys of the movement, who all wear his image on their T-shirts. In defiance of the modernist aesthetic and political values of originality, he insists, with much poignancy, through his interpreter, that his replicated image "gives them a vision they will accept and obey. These children need an identity outside the narrow function of who they are and where they come from. Something completely outside the helpless forgotten lives of their parents and grandparents." They must not be an "invention of Europe." The anonymity of all his children repeats in fearful symmetry the thirteen thousand Moonies married at Yankee Stadium in the opening scene of the novel, DeLillo's nightmare scenario of the end of selfhood: boy-girl pairs so tightly assembled that they are transformed from a "series of linked couples" into "one continuous wave" of potentially frightening force—a mass of people, "approaching division strength," "turned into a sculptured object." In this disturbing linkage of artistic and militaristic metaphors, the mass of people is inert, shapeless material for art, awaiting the shaping hand of the sculptor, who is none other than the Reverend Moon, the only free man: the artist as fascist. All of this to be contrasted with Bill's lost game of self—DeLillo's preferred metaphor of artistic process as the retrieval of innocence, the wholeness of unselfconsciousness, in which the lone (and lonely) individual, through his own imaginative force, transcends his separate self, unlike the passive Moonies, who hand their agony and minds over to their Leader. "The future," as the bleak-toned narrator says, "belongs to crowds"—and to the Father-Fuhrers, like Reverend Moon and Abu Rashid, who manipulate them.

Bill's editor taunts him:

> You have a twisted sense of the writer's place in society. You think the writer belongs at the far margin, doing dangerous things. In Central America, writers carry guns. They have to. And this has always been your idea of the way it ought to be. The state should want to kill all writers. Every government, every group that holds power or aspires to power should feel so threatened by writers that they hunt them down, everywhere.

In the United States, writers don't carry guns; they don't have to. A decent culture offers us freedom of expression, so much the better to ignore serious writers, except on occasions of state dinners, when it is necessary to decorate the table with a poet or two. In Central America, on the other hand, the state wants to kill writers because there writers threaten the state. Bill's idea of the writer as antithesis to power residing in a government or group is touchingly irrelevant: a poising of the artist, champion of free and original selfhood, "one voice unlike the next," against a power that does not feel threatened by novelists. Power in the United States looks out and does not see vivid aesthetic force on a collision course with itself. It looks out and sees Gray.

But what does the Swiss writer-hostage want, for whose body Bill Gray would exchange his own? "The old stories tried and true. . . . The more banal, the more commonplace, the more predictable, the triter, the staler, the dumber, the better. The only thing he didn't have time for was originality." No pleasure, for him, in isolate selfhood, no time for him, no pressing need, for originality. By virtue of his isolation as a hostage in the culture of world terror, he's lost his body, the ground of his real existence, and been reduced to an image circulating through the electronic society. He wants the same fantasies as his brutal guard, this boy, the only one who knows him. He wants to suck on "images that would trail them into middle age, into the final ruin, those sad little picture-stories so dependable and true." Chained to a radiator in a dreary basement, the hostage desires connection to the mainland of human being; connection made possible by narratives that are traditional, that thereby open out to the history of human desire. This is the truth of the "dependable" nonoriginal narrative, the transcending truth of the human dependency that consoles in the time of the final ruin.

In the hostage's situation, DeLillo puts the lie to the fabled opposition of serious artistic culture of the past two centuries—and in so doing suggests his own unspoken alliance to the guarded hope underlying, shyly hidden in, modernist thought and literature. Through the hostage, DeLillo tells us, in effect, that he is having trouble being perfectly sympathetic to his hero, that the choice of a perfectly autonomous (disconnected) selfhood is a choice made inside a society whose alternatives are false and destructive: either selfhood cut off in pain or the prison house of replication. A serious writer, faced with those alternatives, could not but choose isolate selfhood. DeLillo's hostage represents, on the other hand, a desire for community, the kind of collective that nourishes and sustains self within an embracing framework of cooperation and mutuality. The way of isolate selfhood isn't what it seems, isn't the road to freedom and originality but its opposite—another kind of imprisonment.

Consider these normative modernist images of the disconnected self: Dostoevsky's underground man, Eliot's Prufrock and other Waste Landers, Joyce's Stephen Dedalus. Pictures all of fevered consciousness: alienated, self-lacerating and self-loathing; loathsome and lonely. Pictures all of unhappiness and, like Bill Gray himself, sick unto death. Bill's "true biography," appropriately, will be a "chronicle of gas pains and skipped heartbeats, grinding teeth and dizzy spells and smothered breath, with detailed descriptions of Bill leaving his desk to walk to the bathroom and spit up mucus.... Or descriptions ... of Bill staying where he is and swallowing." This is what it means to live as an original, artistic self, pitted against society; it is to live the "solitary life," chained to your writing desk in a room alone, hostage to yourself. You hawk up and spit on your typewriter and produce a monument of writing disease: bloated, unreadable "originality," the counterpart of your own diseased originality of self.

In Bill Gray's description of writing as a process of "self-argument," DeLillo echoes Yeats's exemplary modernist account: that out of the quarrel with others we produce rhetoric, matter for the editorial page, while out of the quarrel with ourselves we create art. It is not Bill Gray, however, who engages in self-argument—he's a relentless spokesman for the values of freedom understood as a function of original (and originating) individuality, of the artist as model of the free man, and perhaps the only free man. It is rather DeLillo himself who engages in self-argument that is irreducible to rhetoric; *Mao II* is his novel, after all, not Bill's, and the text as a whole is a representation of the dramatic swings of his novelistic consciousness: from what would appear to be full-throated support of Bill's aesthetic ideology, to subversive contradiction and sympathy with the Swiss hostage's need to submerge the isolate, sick self in health-restorative community; from celebration of the original self and its artistic expressions to disgust with same (the monstrosity stuck over twenty years in Bill's typewriter). And beyond these agonies of consciousness a vision that the modernized West of materialism, glitz, media blur, and glut cannot fathom and, when it does, cannot abide.

In his opening set piece, "At Yankee Stadium," DeLillo gives us a withering portrait of the yearning to unburden ourselves of "free will and independent thought" (Bill's and ostensibly DeLillo's own highest values) and how happy all those Moony couples are to give it all up, as they chant for "one language, one word, for the time when names are lost" in the great collective dream of Master Moon, who has become "part of the structure of their protein." A mass wedding involving individuals unknown to one another, taking place at Yankee Stadium, where the original American game of athletic virtuosities of self is played, this game, in turn, a figure for the bigger American myth of self—Americans as "grids of pinpoint singularities." In the America of a corrupted Yankee Stadium, in DeLillo's dark apocalyptic suggestion, the game of self will be played no more.

But was Bill's lost game of self, his childhood play of announcing ball games alone in his room, a game of self or was it rather a game of self lost? Self lost in "something larger"? (Bill will abominate that phrase of his secretary and parasite, which echoes T. S. Eliot's account of creativity, community, and salvation.) Is it not, in reality—what Bill describes—a game of the dispersal of the unitary self, propelled out of isolation into the happiness of no-self? "I was the players, the announcer, the crowd, the listening audience and the radio. There hasn't been a moment since those days when I've felt nearly so good." The "I" of the present that does not feel so good, what does it look back on? Surely not "I," happy or other-

wise. He explicates for us: "There's no separation between you and th players and the field. Everything is seamless and transparent." This cannot be the lost game of self that Bill describes because there is no "you" anymore, it's been surrendered to something larger, to a seamless Whole—precisely what Bill will argue against in other passages. Not even Bill knows what he means by "you."

We could call these contradictions "self-argument" were Bill only aware of his internal dissent, but he is not. It is DeLillo who has layered in an exquisite contradiction in the midst of Bill's most romantic memory of childhood, DeLillo who is engaged in self-argument whose subtly suggested resolution will run against his (DeLillo's) most cherished memories of baseball, this very DeLillo who would author American fiction's great love song to baseball in *Underworld*—the novel following *Mao II*—this writer who, in his own voice, in interviews, has affirmed an aesthetic vision of individualism. As a character in *The Names*, an earlier novel, puts it, and which we take as an unusual personal revelation for this writer of the lure of religious vision: "What enormous fears would a man like me have to overcome, what lifelong inclinations to solitude, toward the sanctity of a personal space in which to live and be," in order to "infiltrate Mecca," make the *hadj* with a million and a half pilgrims, and "Surrender." "To burn away one's self in the sandstone hills. To become part of the chanting wave of men." The infinitive form of these fragments—"to burn away," "to become part"—are indications of the speculative embraces (and fears) of desire, not facts of achieved behavior. DeLillo has kept a cautious distance from such desire, put it in the mouths of characters not easily identifiable with himself. Nevertheless, his fiction (from the beginning) displays a reiterative rhythm of such desire, and Bill, a figure of the writer, in some ways close to his author, embodies that rhythm. Bill's primal experience of self-forgetting in his childhood game is the undertow that pushes his narrative course to a place that his conscious mind may not accept, much less be aware of. On his first day in New York in decades, he loves the massive rush of the crowd, "like your first day in Jalalabad." On that day in New York he decides to make a break with his American hermitage and escape from his secretary-parasite-jailer by joining "the surge of the noontime crowd." In Greece, he con-

stantly finds himself lost—in the hotel, in residential areas—he didn't know at times what city he was in. Where is his unconscious taking him? To Lebanon he goes, aboard a ferry bound for Junieh, to exchange himself for the Swiss hostage, but he's dying from a lacerated liver, knows he'll not make it, and DeLillo gives him this last thought: "He wanted devoutly to be forgotten" and will be when his body is rifled for its passport and other identifying papers.

As we read this novel's final sentences, when a chief character in Beirut in the early morning hours mistakes the repeated intense flashes of the white light of high-tech photography for the flashes of cannon fire, and if then we recall Bill's statement to this character, a photographer herself, that the "image world is corrupt," that in a mosque there are no images, and that therefore the "writer who won't show his face is encroaching upon holy turf," we may feel the deep drift, obscure to his own consciousness, of Bill's narrative movement toward self-immolation and (perhaps!) DeLillo's own deepest drift—the resolution of his self-argument, never put into his own voice and words—to see modern Western culture exploded. DeLillo's transgressive desire, like that of many serious artists since Wordsworth, is for a life resting on values not modern (secular, materialist, individualist, liberal) but spiritual. It is also, of course, the desire of the terrorist Rashid—to "complete" the "atrocity" that is the Westernization of the East by literally exploding the West.

Here's the vision:

> There are people gathering in clusters everywhere, coming out of mud houses and tin-roof shanties and sprawling camps and meeting in some dusty square to march together to a central point, calling out a name, collecting many others on the way, some running, some in bloodstained shirts, and they reach a vast open space that they fill with their pressed bodies, a word or a name, calling out a name under the chalk sky, millions, chanting.

That is the apocalyptic culmination of a refrain of images that punctuates *Mao II*—microimages of catastrophe (water-main breaks, explosions outside famous restaurants, a burning sofa, a smoking fuselage in a field, repeated news footage of disasters) and macroimages suggesting an im-

pending shattering of the world as we know it (the mass wedding at Yankee Stadium, the death of Khomeini, Tiananmen Square, the soccer crush at Sheffield, like a medieval painting of suffering done by an old master).

> **Yeats:** Mere anarchy is loosed upon the world,
> The blood-dimmed tide is loosed . . .
> And what rough beast, its hour come round at last,
> Slouches toward Bethlehem to be born?
>
> **Eliot:** Who are these hooded hordes swarming
> Over endless plains, stumbling in cracked earth
> Ringed by the flat horizon only
> Cracks and reforms and bursts in violet air
> Falling towers
> Jerusalem Athens Alexandria
> Vienna London
> Unreal

The apocalyptic vision, be it Yeats's, Eliot's, or DeLillo's, is at once nightmarish—an image of the loss of what is known and valued, for DeLillo a Western ideal of the free individual—and hopeful, an image of destruction of all that is repugnant: for DeLillo that same Western ideal whose pathetic best representative is a novelist self-isolated for more than twenty years in ineffectual autonomy, a freedom of no impact in a world asleep in the postmodern version of savage torpor, induced by the West's image culture of repetition. The transgressive desire beneath many romantic and modernist literary visions is for a terrifying awakening that would undo the West's economic and cultural order, whose origin was the Industrial Revolution and whose goal is global saturation, the obliteration of difference. It is also the desire, of course, of what we are pleased to call terrorism.

"What happens," says Eliot, "is a continual surrender of himself as he is at the moment to something which is more valuable. This progress of an artist is a continual self-sacrifice, a continual extinction of personality. . . . But, of course, only those who have personality and emotions know what it means to want to escape these things."

Bill feels himself impelled to Lebanon because he feels a recognition, the situation speaks to him somehow directly, telling him that he has a destiny and that he must fulfill it. Just before embarking from Greece, he sees a burning tree. Sees but doesn't interpret, perhaps because he can't interpret. He knows and he doesn't know. In Beirut, he's told, he'll be killed by the hostage-takers. To Lebanon then, to sacrifice his life for another. No more the desire—a touch of totalitarian evil, in this novelist-kin to Mao and Moon—to shape mass consciousness. In death, to become so much more than a writer. So it is in his willingness to die for another, not in his failed art, that he surrenders himself to a faith and freedom beyond what can be known by the isolated self—surrenders to something which is larger and more valuable than the horror that he's always known as himself.

3. SOLITARY SAVAGES

In his illness he had dreamed that the whole world was doomed to fall victim to some terrible, as yet unknown and unseen pestilence spreading to Europe from the depths of Asia. Everyone was to perish, except for certain, very few, chosen ones. Some new trichinae had appeared, microscopic creatures that lodged themselves in men's bodies. . . . Those who received them into themselves immediately became possessed and mad. But never, never had people considered themselves so intelligent and unshakeable in the truth as did these infected ones. Never had they thought their judgments, their scientific conclusions, their moral convictions and beliefs more unshakeable. Everyone became anxious, and no one understood anyone else; each thought the truth was contained in himself alone. . . . They did not know . . . what to regard as evil, what as good. People killed each other in some sort of meaningless spite. . . . Only a few people in the world could be saved . . . but no one had seen these people anywhere, no one had heard their words or voices.

CRIME AND PUNISHMENT

+ + +

But here begins a new account, the account of a man's gradual renewal, the account of his gradual regeneration, his gradual transition from one world to another, his acquaintance with a new, hitherto completely unknown reality.

CRIME AND PUNISHMENT

+ + +

Here begins a new account, the account of a man's renewal, a criminal, half Irish, half Chinese, one Rufus (a.k.a. Jack) Henry Abbott, with the help of a famous writer, Norman Mailer, and an ambitious editor at Random House, Errol McDonald; his early transition from one world to another, the account of his rapid degeneration on his acquaintance with a new, hitherto completely unknown reality: the world outside the penitentiary walls. The world inside the penitentiary walls was not unfamiliar to Mailer, author of *The Executioner's Song*, a novel about Gary Gilmore, another career criminal.

It was during Mailer's composition of *The Executioner's Song* that Abbott, a self-described expert on prison violence, first contacted Mailer to offer insight on Gilmore's prison experience. Mailer, no stranger to violence, had stabbed his second wife Adele Morales with a penknife after an all-night party, an act for which she did not press charges. In a recent PBS *American Masters* interview, Mailer discussed this stabbing: "What happened is I was getting into more and more of a violent edge." He cited "dark, ugly and competitive streaks." He said: "We are as ugly as animals in one fashion, and unless we deal with the ugliness in ourselves, unless we deal with the violence in ourselves, the brutality in ourselves, and find someway to sublimate it . . . we're never going to get anywhere with anything."

Abbott emerges from the prison house of repetition a model citizen, the only kind of citizen a totalitarian regime like the American penal system could produce: a highly cultivated criminal. At the end of his sensational book, *In the Belly of the Beast: Letters from Prison*, all letters to Mailer, he predicted his inescapable fate: "I cannot imagine how I can be happy in American society . . . the odds are by now overwhelming that I may not be as other men."

The dystopian community in state and federal penitentiaries, where Abbott grew up, prepared him first for the murder of an inmate and, on his early release at the urging of Mailer and McDonald, for his murder of an innocent waiter outside the Bini-Bon restaurant in New York City on July 18, 1981. The court cited "extreme emotional disturbance" as the reason for the senseless killing—what Abbott called, as he wept at his trial, "one of the most tragic misunderstandings I can imagine." Richard Adan thought he was looking out for passersby, providing Abbott some privacy to urinate in the alley. The Bini-Bon had no restroom. As Adan returned from the street, Abbott thought Adan was about to attack him, so Abbott knifed him in the chest in precisely the way he had so chillingly—and so rivetingly—described his method in his book.

> Here is how it is: You are both alone in his cell. You've slipped out a knife (eight- to ten-inch blade, double edged). You're holding it beside your leg so he can't see it. The enemy is smiling and chattering away about something. You see his eyes: green-blue, liquid. He thinks you're his fool; he trusts you. You see the spot. It's a target between the second and third button on his shirt. As you calmly talk and smile, you move your left foot to the side to step across his right-side body length. A light pivot toward him with your right shoulder and the world turns upside down: you have sunk the knife to its hilt into the middle of his chest. Slowly he begins to struggle for his life. As he sinks, you have to kill him fast or get caught. He will say "why?" Or "No!" Nothing else. You can feel his life trembling through the knife in your hand. It almost overcomes you, the gentleness of the feeling at the center of a coarse act of murder. You've pumped the knife in several times without even being aware of it. You go to the floor with him to finish him. It is like cutting hot butter, no resistance at all. They always whisper one thing at the end: "Please." You get the odd impression he is not imploring you not to harm him, but to do it right.

He worried that he sounded like a "callous punk" for wanting to stop in the middle of this dance of death and "force his life back into him and save him."

A witness reported that Abbott, instead of trying to save Adan, "sadistically taunted" him as he lay dying on the street, killed by a murderer who'd needed instructions on how to read a menu but had written a book on how to use a knife. The murder of the inmate had helped him earn his artistic credentials, his reputation hinging on his ability to describe violence, in letters to Mailer, in an original, enraged voice, the voice of what Mailer called "an intellectual, a radical, a potential leader"—a believer in Marx, Mao, and Stalin, a direct descendent of the pestilence-ridden creatures in the nightmare of Raskolnikov, the hero of Dostoevsky's *Crime and Punishment.* Had Abbott "read himself crazy," as Joseph Frank, in his biography of Dostoevsky, suggests Raskolnikov had? Is he an instance of someone twisting ideologies or twisted by them? Do these ideologies encourage violence of the kind engaged in by Raskolnikov and Abbott? When Abbott committed the crime, Mailer knew he had responsibility for not living with Abbott, newly released from prison, "the way someone in A.A. lives with a drunk," the way a recovering violent offender (Mailer) would live with a criminal who would recover, but has not yet lost his craving for blood, in life as in literature. Here was one criminal ideally situated for a slip.

Prior to his murder of Adan, critics applauded Abbott's writing and his large stature, but after the murder of Adan, *Rolling Stone* cancelled his interview and Doyle McManus of the *Los Angeles Times* regarded him as a "painful curiosity," not an artist. In the modernist tradition, often there is no difference. They couldn't tolerate the elliptical blur between his art and his life, when, after all, his art couldn't exist without his life. Norman Mailer called the fifteen-year sentence Abbott received for causing the death of Richard Adan "a killing." Writing literature had not lifted Abbott out of the purgatory of prison; it had not, as Jerzy Kosinski initially thought, redeemed him from violence. Instead, writing literature had effectively condemned him to death.

+ + +

I wonder, what are people most afraid of? A new step, their own new word, that's what they're most afraid of.

CRIME AND PUNISHMENT

The young gentleman scholar comes to St. Petersburg from the provinces to study the law; the literary antecedent of the Unabomber, another man of words, with educative designs on his society. A year and a half before committing an ax murder, ostensibly in order "to become a Napoleon," he falls under the influence of the radical ideology rampant in the capital. Prior to his radicalization, he'd planned, against his mother's wishes, to marry his landlady's daughter in a supreme gesture of self-sacrifice, a girl described as an ugly, strange invalid—an almsgiver who desired to be a nun. A few months before he leaves the university, his fiancée, with whom he'd argued about his radical views, dies of typhus. In the young man, the impulse for noble self-sacrifice (to his fiancée) and for inspired murder (the pawnbroker and her sister) lay perilously close to each other. When he left the university, six months prior to his murder of the pawnbroker and her sister, and coincident with the onset of a mysterious illness, Rodion Romanovich Raskolnikov (the name evokes the word for schismatic religious dissenter) submitted an article, "On Crime," written in response to a certain unnamed book, to *Weekly Discourse*, which, subsequently, ceased to exist. The origin of the article, his reading of the unnamed book, is theoretical. After Raskolnikov, sick with despair, rejects his friend Razumikhin's good deeds toward him, Razumikhin derides him, in his bookishness, as a thief of other authors' ideas, with no sign of independent life.

According to Raskolnikov's theory, "the act of carrying out a crime is always accompanied by illness," and people are divided into two groups: extraordinary and ordinary. The extraordinary man has the right to commit crimes against someone standing in the way of his "idea," the fulfillment of which would benefit mankind. All lawgivers (like Napoleon) are criminals and do not stop at shedding blood, if it can help them. The ordinary people—conservative, staid—only obey and reproduce. The extraordinary, who speak a new word, destroy the present for the sake of something better, but the masses, who control the present, hang most of these criminals, though future generations of the ordinaries worship them. Some of these extraordinaries escape punishment and triumph in the present. Quite a few, who are ordinaries, and on whom a great joke is played by nature, take it into their heads that they are destroyers of the old word, but these well-behaved cases invariably beat themselves back into submission because that is the law. And, finally, it is the law that there are only very few extraordinaries who have the right to stick in the knife. Raskolnikov merely hints at the idea—made explicit in the Unabomber's *Manifesto*—that shedding blood, *in all conscience*, is permitted. This armed humanitarian had to soften his message in order to get his article accepted.

Unbeknownst to R, the anonymous author of the article, *Weekly Discourse* merged with *Periodical Discourse*, and the "little article," as Porfiry Petrovich, the dissembling prosecutor investigating the crime refers to it, appeared in *Periodical Discourse* two months prior to the murders, where Porfiry had read its dangerous sentences with particular interest. He learned from the editor the secret identity of the obscure, unpaid writer, R, whose original writing was ignored by all but the police.

Dostoevsky imagined Raskolnikov as a grotesque creation of the Russian Nihilists, the men of the 1860s, who with beliefs grounded in the philosophy of utilitarianism and having inhaled the passion for rejection championed by the so-called Westernizers, the men of the 1840s, attacked Russian social institutions as evil. They rejected everything. In place of idealism, they asserted a hedonistic ethics of "rational egoism" or enlightened self-interest—the extreme version of which, let's call it irrational egoism, or unenlightened self-destruction, drove Raskolnikov to utilitarian murder. Writer-intellectual and killer fuse.

This poor, egotistical student, enslaved by poverty and sick with hypochondria, and profoundly disgusted by the world around him, rents a tiny closet like a coffin and lives like a delirious rat in a hole. In debilitating debt to his landlady, his books and notebooks covered with dust, he sleeps without undressing, without a sheet, on his sofa in his coffin, covering himself up with an old coat, his dirty linen bolstering his single, tiny pillow. With no pupils and no means of supporting himself, he takes money from his mother's meager pension and has accepted an advance on his sister's salary as a governess for Svidrigailov, a lifelong slave to Bacchus, who has propositioned Raskolnikov's sister, an ugly circumstance that caused her to leave her job early.

The fact that Raskolnikov had been accumulated into the squalor of the city of St. Petersburg only exacerbated his poverty and purposelessness. With the hairlike worms of this nihilistic egoism, and a full-blown Napoleonic complex festering in his body, Raskolnikov uttered in "On Crime" what he thought was a new word: the shedding of blood is permissible in the service of a greater good. The idea and its scale are supposed to justify stepping over a dead body—destruction of the present in the name of the better. This forefather of criminal artists would jump the gap between word and action. Porfiry worries that people from the lower category, the nongeniuses—those who fear a new word and do not want change—will get it into their heads that they are part of the higher category—those gifted to speak "a new word." This mix-up is precisely what has happened in Raskolnikov's delirious dream in the epilogue of the novel, in which everyone except a few turns into a murderer. An endless repetition of Raskolnikovs, lawless anarchists, populate his dreamscape, where there is no distinction between higher and lower categories of men as he had argued in "On Crime" but, rather, between the pure and chosen who can be saved and those who will not be saved.

During the six months after he penned his article, Raskolnikov lay in a "savage torpor" (like that described by Wordsworth in the preface to *Lyrical Ballads*) doing the work of thinking, the thinking working him finally into a cog in a machine of murder that pulled him along, sapping his will and reason, turning him into a performer, with no control of his actions, in a hideous, but perfectly timed, dream play. "The moment he brought the axe down, strength was born in him." DeLillo's Bill Gray would later say, "There's no longer a moral or spatial distinction between thinking and acting." By contrast, for the Unabomber, the violent acts precede the essay that, he believed, would not otherwise have been published. In Raskolnikov's case, the most important fact about the article, the publication of which comes as a complete surprise sprung on him by Porfiry, is that it implicates him in the murder. It is the single piece of evidence. Urging Raskolnikov to confess, Porfiry promises a reduction of sentence: "Your crime will appear as some sort of darkening." When Raskolnikov does confess, he speaks a "new word" for the first time and "only incoherent sounds came out."

Long before he rises to this "clarity," he is "stoutly lashed on the back with a whip by the driver of a carriage, for almost falling under the horses' hooves even after the driver had shouted to him three or four times"—a drubbing that, according to his article, he richly deserves for presuming to act as a genius when he hasn't the right. A girl with a green parasol puts a twenty-kopeck piece in Raskolnikov's hand out of pity for his beating and beggary. Standing on a bridge with the coin in his hand, he is surprised by a certain unclear, unresolved impression from the splendid panorama of the palace of the tsars, the cathedral dome with four life-size angels shining in the sun, and the blue water—an image that always breathed an "inexplicable chill" on him. "For him the magnificent picture was filled with a mute and deaf spirit"—a spirit not yet uttering a word to him. Throwing the coin in the water, he cuts himself off, as with a scissors, from everyone and everything.

In order to realize his "idea" in "On Crime," Raskolnikov murders the pawnbroker and her sister. His horrifying realization, after he has murdered, is that he's more of a louse than the louse he's axed. Power over the lice of the world! That was to be the endpoint of all his nihilistic smashing. Instead, he comes to see himself as a cowlike creature, a plaything of nature who "imagined" himself a destroyer embodying the new word, who, tormented by his failure to be extraordinary and admitting he only wanted power, finally recognizes Sonya, the prostitute of "insatiable compassion" to whom he finally confesses, as the one who is really "new." "It suddenly came to me, as bright as the sun: how is it that no man before now has dared or dares yet . . . quite simply to take the whole thing by the tail and whisk if off to the devil! I . . . I wanted to dare, and I killed. . . . I just wanted to dare, Sonya, that is the whole reason."

Forced to choose between killing himself and turning himself in to the police, Raskolnikov chooses the latter—a crash from noble self-sacrifice to commitment to Siberian exile and renunciation of political ambition. While ill in prison (in this novel, transformation to good or evil demands illness), he suffers a vivid dream, and love resurrects him from the darkness of his crime. When the dawn breaks, he learns that he had no "idea" behind the murder gives up believing that not the murder but the fact that he did not endure is his crime: he only wanted to kill somebody. Raskolnikov's illness is the fire necessary for him to emerge fully human. If someone came to him now (as happens in Balzac's *Le Père Goriot*), suggesting that he kill an old Chinaman in order to receive a million francs and the fulfillment of all his ideas, he would say with confidence, "I decide to let the Chinaman live."

Like the Unabomber, Raskolnikov is tried on an insanity defense because the world cannot accept the actions of such terrorists as rational. The student of law, the writer, decides to remake his world: "He who can spit on what is greatest will be their lawgiver." To create a new law, to be a Napoleon, you have to break the old one. His weapon of choice is not a bomb—the intellectual's preference—but rather, an ax, artifact of the primitive frontier and symbol of the peasant, the earth, the demonic. He begins as a lethal believer who will kill for faith in nihilism, the forerunner of Marxist-Leninism, and ends as a believer in Dostoevsky's peasant Christian values of love and compassion—with a pastoral vision of freedom, a sun-bathed steppe and nomadic yurts, where time has stopped with Abraham and his flocks. The force that renders Raskolnikov impotent is God.

Dostoevsky had to cross a political line as a member of an antigovernment circle, suffer a mock execution, and go to prison in order to create Raskolnikov, a new man, in order to make his culture see itself: see the extremity, the catastrophic accident waiting to happen, brought about by a combination of Tatar yoke (Asian plague) and Western pressure (nihilism). For Dostoevsky, the only way to freedom is Christian love. The new word, a rupturing originality, held so dear by Raskolnikov, turns out to be the oldest word, the word of God. And the spirit, formerly mute and deaf, of life itself that vanished from his sight when he threw the twenty-kopeck piece into the river is none other than Sonya, who raises him like Lazarus from the dead.

Like the Swiss writer held hostage and tortured in *Mao II*, Raskolnikov, in a Siberian prison camp, tormented by peasants as Dostoevsky was, no longer desires a new word. He desires connection. The isolation Raskolnikov experienced after taking that "new step" of murder was unbearable and ultimately caused him to confess (his only alternative to the path of suicide taken by the depraved Svidrigailov, like Raskolnikov driven by corrupt self-interest, but with no woman to save him). Isolation, prison, salvation. A progression strangely inverted from Joseph Cornell's and Theodore Kaczynski's craft, nostalgia, isolation. From now on his work will be feeling, not thinking.

Raskolnikov's pastoral vision is not unlike the ideal world, a community of free, autonomous individuals, envisioned by Kaczynski who, however, has not suffered the grace of guilt and endured conversion. Raskolnikov's narrative takes him from the study of law and the writing of "On Crime," to murder, confession, and, finally, resurrection. Kaczynski's narrative takes him from his brainwashing in an experiment at Harvard, to acts of mayhem and murder, to writing his *Manifesto* in anticipation of revolution and community, both abruptly interrupted by a life sentence in prison. Just as in the case of Raskolnikov, Kaczynski's acts of violence have led to isolation, an end, not a beginning. Raskolnikov says, "Not only great men, but even those who are a tiny bit off the beaten track—that is who are a tiny bit capable of saying something new—by their very nature cannot fail to be criminals." Dostoevsky says, Raskolnikov must pay for his new life with a great future deed.

The story of Rodion Romanovich Raskolnikov is the story of a murderer with a complex soul, subjected to serial acts of compassion and charity by friends and strangers, men and women alike. But he's a man only confused by those acts, who could not "understand" them—because, he thought, one needed to "deserve" charity and compassion and he, a cold-blooded criminal, did not deserve to be loved. So this literary killer, whose evil deed springs from his reading and writing—tragically out of touch with the kindness in his own nature—cannot fathom the deed that springs not from the reflective and bookish intellect but from the unfathomable and spontaneous heart, the heart that never asks if it has the "right" to act for the good of another but simply does so whenever need reveals itself, as when Raskolnikov himself, without a second's forethought, gives his desperately needed money to the widowed and impoverished wife of a friend.

In the end, Raskolnikov's life of spiritual disablement is shattered by grace. "Here," Dostoevsky says, "begins a new account," of a "man's gradual renewal," "gradual regeneration," "gradual transition from one world to another," and then, having at last embraced his just deserts of compassion and charity, "His acquaintance with a new, hitherto completely unknown reality." It would require another novel, one that Dostoevsky did not write.

+ + +

It's a Martin Scorsese film that we've bought tickets for, and it's called *The King of Comedy.* To this point in his career, 1983, Scorsese's given us (notably) *Mean Streets, Taxi Driver,* and *Raging Bull,* each featuring a violent sociopath played by Robert DeNiro. We know from the advertising that Jerry Lewis has a major role in this one, yet it's DeNiro again (we're sure) who's to be the central figure—this is a Scorsese picture—and therefore we have our doubts that this film will be a comedy in any of the normal senses.

The young DeNiro's art was to disappear into a character, like a monk in contemplation disappearing into God. Nevertheless, it's our habit to say about movies that the star, not the character he plays, said this or did that in the role. It's "DeNiro says," never "Jake LaMotta says." Our habits with novels are different. We say Leopold Bloom does this or thinks that. We don't tend to confuse Bloom with James Joyce. Bloom is merely a character, an illusion of words.

Movies, on the other hand, put those of us out here in Nerdsville—those of us, that is, whose reality quotient in the society of the image is low, at best—into what feels like intimate contact not with characters but with actual famous people. Illusions up there on the big screen—we acknowledge that—but illusions that somehow—we don't know how—give off exhalations of a reality superior to the pathetic real we call our lives. The celluloid world (absurdly) feels hefty, our lives unbearably light. The worlds of fiction, which feature merely characters, cannot offer us what we need, which is why we'd rather go to the movies, or watch television, than read a novel or, if a novel, then those that concern real people, like Mailer's *The Executioner's Song,* or DeLillo's *Libra,* or Capote's *In Cold Blood.*

And now we settle into our seats for this new Scorsese movie, eager for DeNiro to do what DeNiro does. In *The King of Comedy* he too, it turns out, is a celebrity-watcher of tenuous ontological status, who would become a celebrity comedian with the nerdily impossible name of Rupert Pupkin: *mon semblable, mon frère.* Rupert Pupkin: postmodern Everyman, our point of view.

The opening shot of the film is a prerecorded, unedited video image, a filmic image of an electronic image. We're watching a TV show, the very one that the celebrity-hungry Rupert fixates on, about to see someone called Jerry Langford enter, who is clearly intended to represent Johnny Carson, and there's the actual late night TV band leader, Lou Brown, whose character name is Lou Brown, and the actual emcee, Ed Herlihy, whose character name is Ed Herlihy! And we like to say Johnny, and why not? Don't we, after all, say "O.J."? This famous stranger, whom we welcome into our homes nightly, is more than our friend, much more. We've got a crush on him, we're in love, because he is famous, and we are not. Now Johnny himself appears, not as himself (Marty did try to get him for the role), but in the guise of Jerry Lewis (Jerry Langford, Jerry Lewis) and here's Jerry! An actual king of comedy. This movie assumes that we know Jerry Lewis for what he is—a world famous comedian, much watched in his actual life, who in this movie will be put at the mercy of his most obsessive watcher, a lover of sorts, of lethal potential, Rupert Pupkin, who's going to love him like nobody's loved him.

So there we are, in the darkened theater, as in a cave, to watch Robert DeNiro, celebrity, play a celebrity-watcher who is watched from the dark by celebrity-watchers: ourselves. DeNiro in the role we've long wanted him to play: the role of us hungry watchers (a redundancy) who are not all that deluded because we know, we openly acknowledge, that Robert Redford (not at any age) mustn't be cast in this role of ourselves. All Nerds of Nerdsville longing to make contact with a star, take his place in fantasy. Maybe more, maybe actually take his place in the image world and thereby gain at last, in the image world—lie quiet, Plato!—the reality that's been denied us; slough off, at last, this terrible dailiness of our lives.

The pain we experience in the cave of the movie theater is the pain of unrequited love, pain that lies in our need not finally to love but to become our beloved, obliterate who we are and dissolve into one of those images up there on the big screen, disappear into the face of God. Unlike those in Plato's allegory of the cave, our heads are not fettered. We choose not to turn from the images flickering on the wall of the cave and look back to the light and the things of the so-called actual, in the so-called light of the actual, streaming through the cave's mouth. We've been there. We know Nerdsville. We know, alas, ourselves. Only by becoming a celebrated image, we're convinced, will we exist on the enchanted plane of fullness, far above the plane of death in life that we know as desire—desire possessing (as always) what is not. So that's a star then: one who feels no pain of desire. Like God.

Hard cut from the Langford Show to a street scene outside the stage door. A large crowd of autograph hounds, noisy and excited, and there's a man, mustachioed, outfitted in clothes the polyester version of Jerry's, and nerdy white shoes. He's moving with intent through the crowd, he's a known face in the crowd, a celebrity among serial autograph hunters, being asked, as he moves, in a lingo that crosses fans with assassins, if he "got Rodney Dangerfield," and he's responding with a tone of condescension befitting a star, still moving on through, "It's not my whole life. It's not my whole life." This, as it turns out, is a man on a journey precisely to find his *whole* life.

The stage door opens, Jerry appears and the crowd surges dangerously, he can hardly get through to the limo throbbing at the curb. Cut back to the man who didn't get to go to his senior prom, and now we're in slow motion, Jerry's jostled hard as is the senior prom absentee in need of a pink carnation; so much the better, in slow motion and close up, to take in that affectless intensity of the gaze, fixed on Jerry, who doesn't see the mustachioed man coming steadily toward him. Can a star of Jerry Lewis's magnitude be killed off in the opening minutes? We remember Janet Leigh's fate in *Psycho.*

In and outside the movies, this opening scene is uncannily familiar. In the production phase of *The King of Comedy,* Ronald Reagan was shot by a fan—not his, of course, we nerds know John Lennon, and Reagan's no John Lennon, he's just the president of the United States—but a fan of the actress Jodie Foster; shot by one John Hinckley, who was trying to impress the Jodie Foster he'd seen in an earlier Scorsese movie, *Taxi Driver,* whose difference from her character he—a fellow nerd—knows and cherishes, wanting to send her a Valentine, Hinckley was, dipped in the president's blood. The scene of the shooting—a famous man emerging from a building into a crowd surging around him as he moves slowly toward his limo—was replayed countless times on the news, in slow motion; Reagan grimacing as he's hit, then being pushed down into his car by a secret service agent.

The scene in *The King of Comedy* is familiar, too, because we saw its forecast in *Taxi Driver:* DeNiro strapped heavily with handguns—arms, legs, shoes—moving in slow motion, in a crowd, in his Mohawk haircut and army fatigues, toward a presidential candidate. Hinckley playing DeNiro's character in *Taxi Driver,* trying to kill an actual president. Has Scorsese appropriated a historical moment? Is DeNiro, in *The King of Comedy,* playing Hinckley in order to impress the girl he couldn't take to the prom? DeNiro playing Hinckley, who was playing DeNiro: Scorsese's abyss. Later scenes suggest Rupert's need to impress that very girl, Rita she is called, for whom he carried a secret torch. But we nerds can't be fooled at the movies. We've known from the start that this so-called Rita is none other than the actress Diahnne Abbot, Bobby's actual wife. Reagan, a grade-B actor until he got to the Oval Office, where he ascended to the A-plus level, is not JFK; Jerry Langford is not John Lennon. Both survive and two comedies of the 1980s are played out.

As a comedian, Rupert Pupkin is far lower than grade B. In the terms of the visionary metaphor that governs his world, there are only two kinds of people: those who watch TV—the yearners—and those who are on it, who therefore presumably yearn not. Rupert is a watcher; Rupert does not exist. He would become the watched, situate himself in the locus of the real-as-image, the object of yearning that has hitherto governed his life. To practice his art in the only venue that counts—because this venue alone can grant him authentic being—forget the clubs, he's never played a club and never will, he's never played anywhere except in his basement make-believe studio, where he's interrupted only by the abrasive yells of his mom. He's played only in the basement to an audience of himself. So he must—according to Scorsese's psychocultural logic—commit the capital crime of kidnapping, the only direct route from his basement play studio to the Jerry Langford Show, an audience in the multimillions, and requited love at last. He doesn't consider his act a crime, only a justified means to a culturally approved end.

Rupert starts out with petty crimes like harassment and trespassing, in his all-consuming efforts directed (in effect) from the basement of fantasy, where the Jerry Langford Show is his show and Jerry and Liza, in cardboard cutouts, are his guests. (He talks to them. He laughs, tossing back his head in the prescribed manner. He slaps his thigh.) After shedding a little blood in an effort to protect Jerry from the unruly crowd, Rupert slips into the limo with his idol, who reluctantly agrees to let his benefactor ride with him to his apartment. On the way, Rupert offers to take Jerry to lunch, with predictable results, which deter him not. (In the ensuing projected fantasy scene, whose aggressive subtext is palpable, Rupert is a major star and Jerry is begging him at lunch to take over the show for six weeks.) Having made contact, up close and personal, having been given a monogrammed handkerchief by the man himself to stanch the trickle of blood from his finger, Rupert is convinced that he's on an inside track to prime time. (Later he displays the hanky to Rita—like a piece of the shroud.)

In an early scene that reveals the Lewis character in an emptiness of self rivaling Rupert's own, we see Jerry strolling into his apartment after leaving Rupert in his limo with the bloody handkerchief, strolling into a space inhumanly antiseptic and well-ordered, of gleaming floors, and furnishings in steel and glass. As he walks through the entryway, there's a TV monitor playing in his absence and, further on in, a bank of monitors. Jerry lives alone, with a small dog. It is apparently his desire that the monitors play in his absence: it is what he has to come home to. On all of the monitors, a Richard Widmark film is running. Jerry stops at the single monitor, as if he has no choice, as if hailed by commanding force. He watches, lost in fascination, no longer Jerry Langford. America's most watched late night host, who has just left the man obsessed with watching him, is in this moment himself only another isolated watcher, in compelled desire. The phone rings; Jerry picks it up. At the same time, and with his back to the monitor, we see what Jerry cannot: that Widmark is also on the phone, and in the same posture.

Scenes punctuate the narrative at steady intervals, in which Scorsese, in a traditionalist gesture, suggests a context of normal watchers who are not infected with desire to become the object of their gaze, who live in the film century, but whose humanity is not defined by its technology, whose daily acts—like picking up the phone—are not replicants of the world of celluloid and electronic images. They watch playfully, with a modicum of freedom, with a reserve of indifference and boredom. They watch because in the world of this film there is little else to do, but they are not consumed as are Rupert and Jerry. They are the fortunately apathetic citizens of the society of the image, with lives that are independent of the postmodern theater of everyday life.

Rupert takes Rita to a Chinese restaurant. He's showing off his book of autographs. A man walks past, returning to his booth, and sits across from and behind them, looming in the background of the shot, clearly visible. No waiter approaches him. Scorsese's placed him there to watch, as if in a theater, or as if he were sitting before the tube. He begins to mime Rupert—just a little, then all out with gestures of the hands and head and words mouthed in mockery. He seems to be having a very good time, as if to watch a performance requires, for the healthy, not giving a performance before the cameras but giving one on the spot, in the theater of everyday life—as a kind of payback to our fate as watchers. Then he stops, abruptly. Rises and leaves. Playful, then bored. He just walks away. In this microcosmic scene of Scorsese's artistic self-reflection, not the characters but we alone take in the man's performance.

Rupert tries, repeatedly, to see Jerry at his office, with predictable results. He's told by a kindly aide to bring a tape of his monologue, so that they may consider him for a slot. Kindness is again misread. When told that, after auditing the tape, they'd recommend he work the club scene, where they'll catch his act, because they don't think he's quite ready, he says that he'll change the problematic one-liners, no problem. After several of these increasingly pathetic and intrusive occasions, patience runs thin, and he's escorted by security off the premises. Then he learns that Jerry is actually in his office, and the receptionist has lied; Rupert responds by bolting through the reception area toward the suite of offices where Jerry presumably sits in splendid sanctuary. He's apprehended and roughly tossed out on the street.

He becomes only bolder and takes Rita to Jerry's country house in Connecticut, entering without permission, where he's told by the coldly furious celebrity who threatens to call the police, "Has anyone ever told you you're a moron?" As Rupert finally leaves, Jerry calls him an idiot. Cut to a handgun nestled in Rupert's hand. A silent moment. Now (we think) we're in familiar Scorsese territory, but Scorsese has moved from the gritty realism of *Mean Streets* and *Taxi Driver* to the world of simulacra. We hear Rupert's accomplice in crime say, "It looks real." They kidnap Langford at "gunpoint" and as a condition of release—a condition granted—Rupert is permitted to perform his monologue on the Langford Show. Oblivious to FBI threats of violence against his person, he cares only about being made up for his entrance; he will speak only to the producer. But Rupert's crime spree is not over. Before he'll take the FBI agents to Langford (who's already escaped), they must take him to the establishment where Rita bartends, so that he can watch himself on the Langford Show. He doesn't want to take over the show for six weeks. Fifteen minutes of infamy is worth the price of prison time.

He hops up on the bar, and with his hand on the TV, as if on the shoulder of an intimate, and with Rita in attendance, Rupert finds happiness at last when his image flashes on the screen. The beloved-as-imago that he's long sought to become, to extinguish himself in, is not Langford, but himself: postmodern Narcissus; watching himself on TV; watching others watch himself on TV. He has now become his own loving mother, replacing the screamer upstairs, has now properly loved himself and found his "whole" life, or "unity of being," as Yeats put it, beyond the divide of viewer and celebrity, our version of the classic epistemological duo, subject and object.

In that early scene in the limo, Rupert had told Jerry that he knew what he wanted when he saw Jerry take over for Jack Paar. The critical moment for Rupert, for whom there is no authentic life outside the electronic image, is a repetition of Jerry's historic breakthrough. In a prerecorded, unedited video image, precisely the sort of image that had brought Jerry nightly into his home, Rupert Pupkin transcends the death in life of desire that had defined his life outside television.

Traditional Yeats says that "unity of being" is a value of high art in its most intense moment: "O body swayed to music, O brightening glance, / How can we tell the dancer from the dance?" Scorsese, acerbic democrat, responds that in the postmodern moment Yeats's ideal persists but that its locus has shifted to the object of Yeats's considerable contempt, mass culture: here, a trivial late night TV show with presumably nothing in common with high art. The much-touted great divide between traditional culture, a culture of depth and foundations, and postmodern culture, a culture of surfaces—cultivated superficialities of the image—is no divide at all. Yeats: "O chestnut tree, great rooted blossomer. . . ." Scorsese: Oh great rooted television! Rupert Pupkin cannot tell the watcher from the watched: a condition underwritten by his criminal act.

After Jerry has escaped and is making his way back to the studio, he spots a TV monitor playing in a storefront. It's his show, and Rupert Pupkin is filling the screen. He halts, he watches, not in (understandable) anger and disgust but with the entranced gaze of the watcher who doesn't quite inhabit his body. For him, too, the power of the image has suppressed the horror of the crime. The worlds of Rupert and Jerry merge.

But the scene that eventuates in classical comedy's required happy ending of marriage—of Rupert with himself—is not the film's actual ending. The postprison coda, whether fantasy or reality we know not, consists of the transformation of Rupert Pupkin, kidnapper, to Rupert Pupkin, media celebrity. The reward for transgression in *The King of Comedy,* as well as *Taxi Driver,* is fame. Rupert gets a book deal, a movie deal, and a show of his own. Who is the criminal, the culture or the filmmaker? In the wake of having been accused (with *Taxi Driver*) of motivating John Hinckley to shoot Ronald Reagan, Scorsese responds in *King of Comedy* by asking us (in effect) to indict the culture, saturated by media blur and glut, and too eager to reward a criminal act when it becomes a sensational media event.

+ + +

Though there was no television in 1864, the consciousness that emerged as Rupert Pupkin in 1983 was forged more than a hundred years before, in another basement far away from Queens, a basement in St. Petersburg,

Russia, where another morbidly developed young man performed, in language dominated by the books he read instead of the television shows he watched, for an imaginary audience. This other Underground Man, like Scorsese's Pupkin, led a life "solitary to the point of savagery" but lived in a world where class was still determined by birth, money, and military rank, not yet by media celebrity. In Dostoevsky's world, Rupert's coconspirator Masha, instead of finding herself shut out of the halls of television's power and left running around the upper East Side in underwear and heels chasing Jerry, would have held the reins of power by virtue of her birth, money, education, and real estate.

The poverty-stricken Rupert and the Underground Man of Dostoevsky's invention must orchestrate acts of violence to earn recognition from their betters, the "kings": Rupert resorts to kidnapping Jerry Langford for refusing to pay attention to him, and the Underground Man conspires to bump into an officer, the nineteenth-century equivalent of a media star, who treated him like a fly. These morbidly developed drones who conspire to dramatically transcend their pathetic circumstances would force their stars to take notice of them and fulfill their fantasies of friendship. The Underground Man's servant Apollon persistently pierces his basement bubble illusion of himself as a player. Rupert's mother routinely interrupts his belowground-level star turn with infantilizing shouts objecting to his volume and summoning him to the bus and his unglamorous job as a messenger boy. In fantasy, Rupert would marry Rita, the barmaid, on network television, after receiving a long overdue apology from his high school principal (both heroes suffered the equivalent of penal servitude in school), and the Underground Man would rescue the prostitute from debasement if only Apollon weren't there to remind him of his inescapable fly-like status. In reality, both men cannot help abusing these women when they inadvertently get in the way of their true goal.

Television has taught Rupert what he wants to do with his life: take over for Jerry as Jerry took over for Paar. The new king will replace the old, in a hostile takeover if necessary, in this aristocracy of the image world. The Underground Man embraces his world-rejecting, embittered autonomy by remaining in his basement—a condition not unlike the final hallucinatory image of Scorsese's film, where the silent and inward-gazing Rupert inhabits, in solitude, before an audience like the one pictured in his fantasy, an eternal pause.

+ + +

Civilization cultivates only a versatility of sensations in man . . . and through the development of this versatility, man may reach the point of finding pleasure in blood.

NOTES FROM UNDERGROUND

Both the author of these *Notes* and the *Notes* themselves are, of course, fictional. Nevertheless, such persons as the composer of these *Notes* not only exist in our society, but indeed must exist, considering the circumstances under which our society has generally been formed. I have wished to bring before the public, somewhat more distinctly than usual, one of the characters of our recent past. He represents a generation that is still living out its days among us.

FYODOR DOSTOEVSKY, _NOTES FROM UNDERGROUND_
(EPIGRAPH TO _AMERICAN PSYCHO_)

In the epigraph to Bret Easton Ellis's notorious novel *American Psycho,* Dostoevsky asserts the necessity and inevitability of people like the writer of *Notes from Underground,* whose existence is owed to "the circumstances under which our society has been formed." Ellis, thereby, invites comparison between St. Petersburg in the 1860s and Manhattan in the 1980s, between the Writer (of the Notes) and Patrick Bateman, antihero and Psycho of America—representative of a new generation "still living out its days among us."

There's a story here: the deterioration of an intellectual/artist figure from the nineteenth century, with a desire for domination, who humiliates because he's been humiliated, who commits mental cruelty, who wars with the ever-shredding impulses of his morality. The Underground Man delightedly turns to writing literature to describe an officer who while moving him bodily from one place to another because he was blocking the way, nevertheless fails even to notice him, treats him "like a fly." *Fatherland Notes* declined to publish his exposé of the officer, however, because there were, as yet, no exposés. The Underground Man was penalized for creating an original literary form.

Dostoevsky's artist-figure degenerates into a Harvard, prep school–educated, trust-funded Wall Street executive who hasn't enough aesthetic sensibility to hang his very expensive painting right side up. In fact, he tortures and kills an ex-girlfriend who has the misfortune of pointing this out. Or does he, in fact? Since we can no more rely on Bateman' s notes (or rather, lists) than the Underground Man's, the question of whether this particular psycho (his mental instability is never in question) actually commits any of the crimes he so painstakingly details, is decidedly up for grabs. This aesthete of capitalism, guilty of a sensuous grasp of the surfaces of the most expensive commodities, may be slapping these crimes on himself solely out of vanity.

Bateman is a writer in the sense that these first-person notes/lists are his: he has written them. He is also a director in that he instructs the camera that his eyes have become to pan, cut, zoom, dissolve slowly, smash cut, lapse time. His life is a movie. The Underground Man stifles what boils up inside of him with the external sensations of literature, the so-called lofty and beautiful, in novels and poems that he reads at home, fully aware of their alienating and debasing influence, aware that the books he reads generate his behavior and turn him into a mechanical creature. Bateman keeps any feelings, other than vanity and the desire to dominate, suppressed by inhaling things vulgar and vile with seemingly no awareness of their influence, falling into romance with image over reality, losing what little self of him there is to begin with to the garbage of his own culture: videos, CDs, television, porn.

Having something to watch (his image, TV, videos, etc.) saves Bateman from reflection, the very thing that is the Underground Man's unrelenting source of pain. Ellis cleverly arranges for his repressed-homosexual misogynistic hero, armed with his hard-core porn mags and sporting a bloody nose, to be joined in the elevator by Tom Cruise, often accused of being a homosexual. To the doorman, Bateman is a ghost, unreal, intangible—he possesses all the qualities of an image, not a human being. Cruise, much shorter in person, possesses (paradoxically) more reality, more tangibility than Bateman ever could because of his celluloid stardom.

Here it is, here it is at last, the encounter with reality.

NOTES FROM UNDERGROUND

Both Bateman and Dostoevsky's Writer look upon themselves with furious dissatisfaction, attribute their view of themselves to everyone else, and suffer extreme anguish as a result. They do not sleep. Even though Bateman is continually mistaken for someone else—the Wall Street denizens in Ellis's novel are virtually indistinguishable from one another—Bateman feels as if no one else is like him. Neither Bateman nor the Underground Man can forgive people for not noticing them. For the Underground Man, the way to encounter reality is through slapping somebody, bumping into someone on the street, using cruel language. For Bateman, one hundred and twenty years of civilization have taught him that he needs to carry his violent impulses a good deal further to get the proper notice. Ellis, the author, may have suffered from the same malaise in writing this work.

American Psycho never begins to approach the structural perfection of Dostoevsky's novella, in the first part of which the Writer describes himself, his views, and tries to illuminate the cause of his existence; the second, twenty years earlier, the actual notes, concerns certain events in his life. *American Psycho* is a bloated literalization or vulgarization of *Notes from Underground,* with Bateman acting out the literary metaphor of the Underground Man. At the end of the *Notes,* the Underground Man accuses his interlocutor, "I have merely carried to an extreme in my life what you have not dared to carry even halfway." Bateman could say the same thing to the Underground Man. Both want to be "living," and violence is the ticket to "where the living lives now."

American Psycho begins with an unnamed Bateman, in camera mode, setting the scene in one very long sentence/shot, and coming to rest on his colleague Tim Price. Commonly regarded as the boy next door, Bateman sees himself reflected in Price and in any and all available glass surfaces, dwelling as he does in an extreme of self-consciousness, starving for external confirmation. To experience himself, he must see an image of himself and he—unlike the Underground Man—likes the surface of what he sees.

> By chance I looked in a mirror. My agitated face seemed to me repulsive in the extreme: pale, wicked, mean, with disheveled hair. "Let it be; I'm glad of it," I thought, "I'm precisely glad that I'll seem repulsive to her; I like it. . . ."
>
> ***NOTES FROM UNDERGROUND***

The only way that Bateman—obsessed with reading biographies of the serial killer, Ted Bundy, and whose biggest concerns are getting reservations at hip restaurants, being seated at good tables, and figuring out what to order—distinguishes himself from his colleagues is by acts or, at the very least, thought crimes of vicious, usually racist or misogynistic, mayhem. Bateman's fear that his new business card is not superior to those of his fellow homophobic boys club colleagues transforms him into a monster whose hands have minds of their own. Temptation to kill changes to desire to drink champagne and gratify himself instantaneously, as if his mind were a TV set whose channels were surfed by an unknown third party.

Mistaken identity plagues this character, whose deepest frustration is his lack of recognition by outside parties. Here is a man who spends so much time dressing well (he's an encyclopedia on correctness), coiffing well, buffing well, killing well, that he's disappeared somewhere inside the act that is himself. Like Dostoevsky's Underground Man, he does not exist. No one takes him seriously except when he's about to kill her. Hence, his need for the identity fix.

The Underground Man knows he's trash, can't stand himself, and is scared. What about Bateman? He has some lint of morality on his Brooks Brothers topcoat, but the shreds are ultimately buried beneath the debris Ellis relentlessly piles up detailing various crimes. The novel, as the confession of a 1980s yuppie consumer–serial killer, met mainly with critical disgust.

> They won't let me. . . . I can't be . . . good!
>
> ***NOTES FROM UNDERGROUND***

Dostoevsky began *Crime and Punishment,* after *Notes from Underground,* as a first person confession (like Ellis's novel) by the antihero, Raskolnikov. Discarding this approach as too narrow and confining, he fashioned the brilliant third-person narration that still allowed for Raskolnikov' s fevered interior episodes. Ellis, dubious master of disgusting repetition and excess, suffers the limitations of first-person narration in his, at times, brilliant work but does not reap the advantage of the form: the capacity of the narrator to be a critical observer as well as a participant in the narrative.

Poverty created the Underground Man's vanity: "I'm so vain it's as if I'd been flayed and the very air hurts me." The vanity of Bateman—slave to adrenaline rushes and victim of constant tension—seems culturally induced. His desire to fit in drives the endless lists of products that should help fulfill that desire but, instead, only form an inch-thick icy crust over his head, keeping him numb and half frozen beneath the surface, struggling to break on through to the other side. Bateman has wealth and position, but no one to care if he disappears into that crack above the urinal's handle.

The period of the 1840s, like our own 1960s, was characterized by sublime, beautiful, humanitarian ideas. The 1860s, like the 1980s—the Reagan-Bush era—revealed a utilitarian antiaesthetic. "There wasn't a clear, identifiable emotion within me, except for greed. . . . I had all the characteristics of a human being—flesh blood skin hair—but my depersonalization was so intense, had gone so deep, that the normal ability to feel compassion had been eradicated." Wall Street, the ideal structure for utopian capitalist society, is a kind of equivalent of Dostoevsky's Crystal Palace, a structure of cast iron and glass—"the ideal living space for the future utopian communist society" (*Notes from Underground*).

> For without power and tyranny over someone, I really cannot live. . . .
>
> ***NOTES FROM UNDERGROUND***

Bateman's racist knife attack on a bum, whom he accuses of faggotry, is as intimate and brutal as Raskolnikov's ax murder of the pawnbroker and her sister. It's personal, not business. Like Raskolnikov's victim, the pawnbroker, the bum is a parasite, but the economic positions of murderer and victim are reversed. Pawnbroker has money Raskolnikov needs. Bum needs money Bateman has. After creating his humorous tableau of the crime, Bateman, "ravenous, pumped up," heads to his victim's restaurant, none other than McDonald's, persistent symbol of American capitalism's domination of the world market.

Bateman is plagued by anxiety attacks. No one hears what he says. When he says "murders and executions" people hear "mergers and acquisitions." He sets up a Sony palm-sized Handycam to film his acts of misogynistic murder. On planet Bateman, not only does he behave as if in a film but his victims do, too. They move in slow motion. He doesn't know if he's awake or dreaming: "I am so used to imagining everything happening the way it occurs in movies," just as to the Underground Man everything happens the way it occurs in literature.

I was no longer able to love . . . for me to love meant to tyrannize and to preponderize morally.

NOTES FROM UNDERGROUND

What can we say about Patrick Bateman—that he was a closet homosexual who did a lot of cocaine? Characterizing himself as empty, devoid of feeling, but still possessing his senses, he's not so vacant that he doesn't know he's vacant. Ellis juxtaposes an endless repetition of major air disasters on TV with Bateman's use of new deodorant. Bateman, though sorely lacking a critical stance toward Wall Street, refuses to accommodate himself in strange and senseless ways to the Waste Land according to Reagan, doing nasty things to exercise his free will while gaily accepting supply-side trickle-down economics in all its implications. Bateman is Deregulated Man, and Ellis's novel is the full-blown realization of a vision of America articulated by Svidrigailov in *Crime and Punishment:* a place where one can commit ax murders with impunity. Here, civilization has made mankind harder, consequently more bloodthirsty and better fitted for warfare.

Give him some economic prosperity so that he has nothing else to do but sleep, eat cakes, and busy himself with ensuring the continuation of world history—even then man, out of sheer ingratitude, sheer slander, will play you some dirty trick.

NOTES FROM UNDERGROUND

It all ends with a whimper—a kind of dirty trick perpetrated by Ellis. Imagine Bateman as Peter Lorre as "M," hunted down and tried by the cabdrivers downtown in the bowels of Manhattan. Or Jean, his secretary, could become his Sonya, restoring him as a human being. Were Bateman to reject videos, TV, and CDs, to what soil should he return? Christianity as a restorative ideal does not exist in this American world where the spiritual authority is capitalism. The cabdriver who catches up with Bateman, the murderer of his friend, is a cheap date, his justice bought off with a Rolex replaced the next day by Bateman's insurance company. Imitating reality, Bateman, like most serial killers, just goes on and on without ever being caught. Finally, like Peter Lorre in *M*, who is filled with self-loathing, he kills a child. Bateman says, "This thing before me, small and twisted and bloody, has no real history, no worthwhile past, nothing is really lost"—a projection of Bateman's true self.

Somehow he progresses from having some erratic, inconclusive instances of conscience to having none, no doubt as a result of Aristotelian logic: by continuing to commit gratuitous excessive acts of violence, if only in his mind, he loses whatever shred of humanity lingered. He proceeds to virtual absence of humanity. As his fiancée Evelyn so accurately attests: he has no right to be so embittered, his animosity is grounded on nothing. There must be something the matter with him. But what is it exactly? Is it him or is Ellis blaming the social conditions that must inevitably produce him? Ellis offers up the product lists, like the detailed descriptions of murders and endless essays on careers of various pop stars (ultimately unreadable) as the cause, the cause, my soul. How can such a rich, overeducated garbage brain become anything else but a serial killer? His need to engage in homicidal behavior is the only way he can express his "blocked . . . needs." As he descends into cannibalism, he realizes killing is his only reality, which he must film. "Everything outside of this is like a movie I once saw." His conscience, pity, hopes all disappeared at Harvard—an ominous echo of what happened to Theodore Kaczynski.

Ellis falls fatal victim to the imitative fallacy: in writing about an antihero devoid of feeling, who spews lists of products and pop music trivia and overdoses on violent acts, he's written a novel devoid of feeling, has spewed lists of products and pop music trivia, and overdosed on violent acts. Even a red pen couldn't solve the problem of the lack of catharsis, the lack of a gain on the part of Bateman or the reader of any deeper knowledge about him. "No new understanding can be extracted from my telling. There has been no reason for me to tell you any of this. This confession has meant nothing. . . ." Of course, Ellis would say that was precisely his point, that Bateman's persistent making of his life into the art of a movie indicates his need for a life of meaning, with form and resolution, and events proceeding according to rules—the kind of life that does not exist in the world according to Ellis.

What's more, anguish kept boiling up; a hysterical thirst for contradictions, contrasts, would appear, and so I'd set out on debauchery.

NOTES FROM UNDERGROUND

Bateman and his creator suffer from postindustrial numbing: two hundred plus years of mechanization of humanity, overcrowding, alienation from nature, inundation by news, and habituation to the artistic equivalent of cattle prods, causing them to seek impact—artistic and otherwise—through excessive violence. Both suffer from the "savage torpor" identified by Wordsworth, who foresaw the problem these Wall Street types, with their uniformity of occupations and accumulation in cities, would have: "a craving for extraordinary incident." Wordsworth laments "this degrading thirst after outrageous stimulation" as evil. Ellis, however, does not number among those artists anticipated by Wordsworth, who would oppose this evil systematically. On the contrary, in spite of his gifts, he wallows inexorably in the muck. Ellis achieved impact with his work but probably not the kind he desired. Critical reaction to the novel, including condemnation even prior to publication, was damning. The Los Angeles chapter of the National Organization of Women boycotted Vintage, the publisher, and Knopf, its parent.

I guess the book is an expression of my feelings of how I felt the 1980s went awry, went astray, went crazy. . . . The consumerist excess. The total compulsive fascination with surfaces. How everyone was defined by what they wore, what they bought, rather than who they were.

ELLIS, *RENO-GAZETTE-JOURNAL*

As Joseph Frank points out in his biography of Dostoevsky, the critic Mikhailovsky, in his article "A Cruel Talent," cites sadistic passages from *Notes from Underground* and argues that they illustrate Dostoevsky's own "tendency to torture." Likewise, Christopher Lehmann-Haupt comments on the "lack of ironic distance between [Ellis's] own voice and that of his psychopathic narrator." In both instances, satirical parody has been misunderstood and taken straight. As a satiric figure, Bateman, the "I" narrator, is a convention and not meant to be taken as a genuine character, but his psychological presence and the force of his violence, against women in particular, works against that depersonalization.

Only Henry Bean recognized the novel as "a satire, a hilarious, repulsive, boring, seductive, deadpan satire of . . . the Age of Reagan." Calling Ellis a "moralist," he differentiates Bateman's crimes from Jean Genet's: Bateman is not revolting to gain freedom but rather to gain retribution. "*American Psycho* tells of the greed and soullessness," initiated by Nixon and fulfilled by Reagan and the Bushes, "that leads inexorably to gratuitous murder." Dostoevsky's prediction in *Crime and Punishment* of the advent of an amoral world inhabited by people who kill each other "in some sort of meaningless spite" is fully realized in the nonfiction life of Jack Henry Abbott and the fictional world of *American Psycho.*

When Jean-Luc Godard "was making his first feature film, 'Breathless' (1959), he is said to have asked what the convention was about the maximum camera swing acceptable to the eye in a single shot. He was told that it was a hundred and eighty degrees. He immediately asked his cameraman, Raoul Coutard, to use a great deal more."

This offense is called "crossing the line."

JEAN-LUC GODARD INTERVIEWS

4. CROSSING THE LINE

After six years in the Indian Ocean, the Pacific, and the China Seas, Charley Marlow—figure of the modernist writer, a teller of so-called inconclusive tales—returns home to London with (as he puts it) a "regular dose of the East," to rest and loaf about with friends—"hinder" them at work and "invade" their homes. His friends? The Director of Companies, the Lawyer, and the Accountant: men with high places in a British firm granted concessionary rights in Africa (along with the French, Dutch, and Portuguese), granted imperial freedom, by Leopold II of Belgium, to extract product in the lucrative ivory trade, in the Congo, and bring progress of the moral sort to the native born.

When he tires of resting in London, and thanks to the help of a well-connected insider—an aunt living in Brussels, with ties to the most powerful authority in the General Administration of the Congo—Marlow succeeds in securing an appointment to captain a steamer deep into the interior. As *Heart of Darkness* opens, we find him aboard the *Nellie,* a yawl cruising on the Thames, poised—as he sits in the lap of luxury—to tell the story of a man named Kurtz to an audience of old intimates: the

Lawyer, the Accountant, an unnamed frame narrator, and their host, the yawl's gracious owner and captain, the Director of Companies himself.

Marlow tells of his struggle to meet Kurtz and various awful sights of colonial progress along the way—Kurtz, the agent held in highest esteem by the Belgian Prime Movers of Extraction. Marlow would relieve Kurtz of an immense load of booty, but also—and at least as important—fulfill a dream he'd had when just a "little chap" with a "passion for maps": to explore what he's pleased to call the "blank spaces" on the earth, so much the better to satisfy a "hankering," he says, in words that Conrad will repeat a decade later in an autobiographical book—a "hankering" for the "biggest, the most blank," the dark continent itself.

After the devastating experience of meeting Kurtz, about whom we never learn very much, Marlow returns to Brussels, then finally to London, the "monstrous town," as the frame narrator calls it, still recuperating from a difficult illness contracted in the jungle (as had Conrad), to rest, hinder his friends once again, invade their homes, dine and live with them, and tell his story. Interrupted in the midst of his caustic narrative, and asked to be "civil," he's rebuked, in effect, as an ingrate guest, whose asides to his audience bite the hand that feeds.

Nevertheless, this well-connected, sometimes ungrateful narrator called Marlow, always comes home (ideologically as well as geographically) to monstrous London, and the hand that feeds. Unlike Huck Finn, he has no desire to "light out for the territory."

+ + +

> There was a sense of extreme disappointment, as though I had found out I had been striving after something altogether without a substance. I couldn't have been more disgusted if I had traveled all the way for the sole purpose of talking with Mr. Kurtz. Talking with . . . I . . . became aware that that was exactly what I had been looking forward to—a talk with Kurtz. I made the strange discovery that I had never imagined him as doing, you know, but as discoursing. . . . The man presented himself as a voice. Not of course that I did not connect him with some sort of action. Hadn't I been

> told in all the tones of jealousy and admiration that he had collected, bartered, swindled, or stolen more than all the other agents together? That was not the point. The point was in his being a gifted creature, and that of all his gifts the one that stood out preeminently, that carried with it a source of real presence, was his ability to talk, his words—the gift of expression, the bewildering, the illuminating, the most exalted and the most contemptible, the pulsating stream of light, or the deceitful flow from the heart of an impenetrable darkness.

So Marlow, who reveals, without knowing that he does, the story of himself by telling the story of Kurtz. We'll call the unnamed and shadowy framing narrator of Marlow's story "Conrad," with insistence on the quotation marks. Conrad (without quotes), the name that appears on the title page, splits himself into two narrators—"Conrad" and Marlow, his autobiographical projection, for the purpose—this is the desire—of insulating himself from complicitous involvement in the project of imperialism. Against all of Conrad's considerable novelistic guile, it is a contamination that he cannot keep his text from revealing to us. Like Marlow, Conrad-without-quotes will tell the story of himself but without knowing that he does so.

Marlow has almost made it to the Inner Station, where Kurtz reigns, when he's told that Kurtz is no doubt dead—"something," after all, "altogether without a substance." When he does finally see Kurtz, alive but at the edge of death, he describes him as a culmination of the various important—and inhuman—representatives of imperial business whom he's encountered on his journey to the interior: one man, the Company's chief accountant, dressed like a "hairdresser's dummy"; another, the manager of the Central Station, who has "nothing within him," and declares that "men who come out here should have no entrails"; and still another described as a "papier-mâché Mephistopheles," with "nothing inside but a little loose dirt"—all of these men, in words that Marlow will soon deploy to evoke Kurtz, are "hollow at the core."

Like Melville's Ahab (a pre-Kurtz with a chest that rings like a "hollow metallic barrel"), Fitzgerald's Gatsby (a post-Kurtz who appears to "leak sawdust"), and Eugene O'Neill's Hickey (New York City's chief illusion distributor), Conrad's Kurtz has a long-deferred entrance, prefigured with tantalizing hints: he's a poet, a painter, a musician, a journalist—a figure, no less, of the artist-intellectual. And "all Europe," Marlow says, "contributed to the making of Kurtz." As the production, the very secretion of Europe (his hollow cultural parent) Kurtz is Europe's voice, Europe's artist-intellectual and cultural enforcer. And of all the arts that he practices, his ability to "electrify large meetings" is the one that best represents his expressive powers and the political core of his identity. His force of public eloquence—Marlow insists repeatedly on the eloquence of Kurtz's voice—would have made him a popular politician, of an "extreme party." *Which* party, Marlow asks, and the answer he's given is definitive for the politics of hollow men: "Any party . . . He was an—an—extremist." This "gifted creature" Kurtz, gifted most with the "bewildering" "gift of expression," bewilders Marlow and Conrad himself, the hapless writer as Dr. Frankenstein, who created Marlow and Kurtz. Kurtz expresses: he "presses out." He is eloquent—speaks out with force and passion. But presses out and speaks out of what? What if not his hollowness at the core?

Marlow is sardonically knowing about imperialism's rhetorical patina. He spits out relentlessly, and fiercely, the eloquent phrases of imperial business, like "glorious idea," "noble cause," "progress," "knowledge," "emissaries of light," "weaning the ignorant millions from their horrid ways," "philanthropic desire," "pity," and "science." He pronounces it all "rot." The mission of Europe in Africa is to fill the unfillable hollowness at the core, simply to eat, by practicing the "merry dance of death and trade."

So the art of empire, which is Kurtz's mouth of eloquence, and from which pours the "pulsating stream of light," at the same time is the mouth of voracity. The mouth that says, "My intended, my ivory, my station, my river, my—" "everything," says Marlow, "belonged to him." "I saw him open his mouth wide—it gave him a weirdly voracious aspect, as though he had wanted to swallow all the air, all the earth, all the men before him." As Kurtz is borne to the steamer, Marlow says: "I had a vision of him on the stretcher, opening his mouth voraciously . . . a shadow insatiable of splendid appearances, of frightful realities; a shadow darker than the shadow of the night, and draped nobly in the folds of a gorgeous eloquence."

Clear enough, Marlow *knows:* sees through Kurtz into the nasty business of empire. Or is it best to say that *this* Marlow, but only in *these* moments, is empire's adversarial narrator? What are we to make of the Marlow who, on encountering the Eldorado Exploring Expedition, says that "there was not an atom of foresight or of serious intention in the whole batch of them, and they did not seem aware these things are wanted for the work of the world. To tear treasure out of the bowels of the land was their desire, with no more moral purpose at the back of it than there is in burglars breaking into a safe." These so-called explorers were just "sordid," "greedy," and "cruel." *This* Marlow (guest of the Director of Companies) seems to have forgotten, or never to have made the acquaintance of, himself as savage undoer of imperial rhetoric. This Marlow is the dupe of imperial rhetoric, a man who needs to make a distinction between Kurtz's gift of expression and Kurtz's bloody actions, not knowing what the other Marlow knows: that Kurtz's expressive gift of eloquence is the high, "contemptible" literary drapery of his actions on behalf of the Company. This Marlow, enthralled by Kurtz's gift, needs to believe that Kurtz's final words, "The horror! The horror!" constitute a last moral testament: a devastating judgment on all that he, in the name of the Company, has done. The other, the acerbic Marlow knows that Kurtz's manuscript—which began, "By the simple exercise of our will we can exert a power for good practically unbounded"—had ended with what our deadpan storyteller calls the "exposition of a method" for actualizing the benign immensity of his intentions: that famous scrawled postscript, "Exterminate all the brutes!"

The fissured narration of Marlow, a character at odds with himself, is in evidence virtually everywhere in *Heart of Darkness.* Like a politically leftward-tending member of the academic community, he believes in the incommensurability of cultures and the futility of a universal standard. The sound of drums in the night causes him to think that they have "as profound a meaning as the sounds of bells in a Christian country," and though he is forever (and necessarily) shut off from that meaning, seems willing to let it alone, honor its difference. When the starving cannibals on board his steamer will not kill and eat the White men, himself included, Marlow concludes that they have "restraint," his crucial term for describing the ultimate civilizing trait, the withholding, the holding in, of the natural urge. He notes, comically, that they, the Whites, may look—being White—unappetizing. From the point of view of another cultural standpoint, disgusting. No matter: "restraint" is precisely, he says, what Kurtz lacked, who was thereby, this finest representative of European enlightenment, a mere natural thing at the mercy of natural forces, "a tree swayed by the wind"—the truest of savages.

Black culture in the Congo is equal in humanity to the White Christian culture of Europe. Or: Blacks are in need of the moral doctrine that Europeans bring in order to lift Blacks to full human status. Which is it? Blacks are the truly civilized; Kurtz is an animal. Or is it the other way around?

The multiple and incompatible interpretations of Marlow cannot be resolved by appeal to dialectical principle. There is no deeper, or higher, coherence of Hegelian Idea—unless it inhabits some aesthetic principle, a style of narrating that embraces, without resolving, contradictions and incompatibilities. Perhaps the art of Marlow's telling operates beyond his fissured understanding. Perhaps his art knows more than he knows. The framing narrator, "Conrad," gives us a handle:

> The yarns of seamen have a direct simplicity, the whole meaning of which lies within the shell of a cracked nut. But Marlow was not typical . . . and to him the meaning of an episode was not inside like a kernel but outside, enveloping the tale which brought it out only as a glow brings out a haze. . . .

"Inside" *Heart of Darkness,* at its heart: Kurtz, dry hollow kernel, but a fascinating hollowness. The "fascination of the abomination"—the phrase is Marlow's, and it describes, at the outset of his tale, a "decent young citizen in a toga," in the service of empire (Roman)—an ancient precursor of Kurtz, reacting (as Marlow imagines him) to the savagery of "some inland post," in the heart of darkness that was (and still is, according to "Conrad") Britain. Marlow, as Nietzschean historian, implies that

Kurtz's story is only the latest episode of a repetitious history of domination and iniquities of power and wealth. In this gloomy metaphysics of history, the future is the past, the present a misnomer, and opposition a futile gesture against the way things have been and always will be in all societies, regardless of racial differences.

"Outside" the dry hollow kernel that is Kurtz, there's Marlow's narrative style, those astonishingly elastic sentences of his, that envelop the story of Kurtz—sentences often long, convoluted, excited—and commanding the amazing gamut of his reactions to the object of his fascination.

> The point was in his being a gifted creature, and that of all his gifts the one that stood out preeminently, that carried with it a sense of real presence, was his ability to talk, his words—the gift of expression, the bewildering, the illuminating, the most exalted and the most contemptible, the pulsating stream of light, or the deceitful flow from the heart of an impenetrable darkness.

"The point was": this sentence will deliver a point, seems to promise that most un-Conradian "direct simplicity" of the average seaman's yarn. "A gifted creature," and of all his gifts, one stands out; it is, apparently, "the point": Kurtz's "ability to talk." Why not stop there? "His words"—certainly *those* words are not required: we've just been told that Kurtz is a great talker. "His talk," "his words." In such repetition we move to a level of expressive gift and affect, Marlow's, as he recollects entrancement, his own. He's beginning to stutter. Perhaps the real point is his entrancement, but if it is, it's a point he's not capable of making. "His talk," "his words," "the gift of expression." Marlow is fixated. And then the deep plunge, the effort to describe Kurtz's gift: "the bewildering, the illuminating"—serially? or at the same time?—"the most exalted and the most contemptible"—separable qualities, or is "the point" about Kurtz that he's bewildering because these qualities are, as the conjunctive "and" suggests, simultaneous? "Pulsating stream of light," or "the deceitful flow from the heart of an impenetrable darkness?" Light and dark: obsessive images in this novella, a classic literary opposition, but can they be segregated in Kurtz's gift? Or is enlightenment (as the Unabomber, a reader of

Conrad, thinks) the final darkness? And is *this* the source of Kurtz's (and imperialism's) charismatic power: his (its) ability to paralyze, at once to appall and attract, and thereby clog understanding and judgment, Conrad's, Marlow's, and ours? Entrancement; enthrallment; identification. Scorn; disgust; irony; cynicism. Those are the schizoid tones of *Heart of Darkness*, and Marlow, their agonized voice, is at once Kurtz's severe critic and a Kurtz idolater. If no clear-sighted opposing of Kurtz, then no opposition to Europe. No transgressive act of art is possible.

"Outside" Marlow, the framing narrative voice of "Conrad," and sentences that sometimes do not so much frame, objectify, or distance Marlow for our contemplative pleasure as mirror his literary style, suck us (and "Conrad") in: "Hunter for gold or pursuers of fame, they had all gone out on that stream [the Thames], bearing the sword, and often the torch, messengers of might within the land, bearers of a spark from the sacred fire."

The theory of the Marlovian narrative is modernist: meaning lies not in an isolable and extractable (kernel-like) center, but in the total enveloping "haze" of the aesthetic texture of the whole—the image colors, the peculiar diction, the syntax, the special swing of the sentences. A totally enclosed, autonomous, and entrapping aesthetic "experience." No "meaning." No isolable statement of any kind, much less one concerning the evils of imperialism.

This narrative theory of aesthetic autonomy that would explain the self-enclosed art of *Heart of Darkness* is echoed in three distinctly isolable thematic moments. The steamer that takes Marlow up river to fetch the gravely ill Kurtz must be repaired before the journey can properly begin. To this point, Marlow tells us that he's been subjected to a variety of rumors about Kurtz and to violent spectacles of physical abuse of the Blacks. Need to work on the steamer comes as a relief: "I went to work the next day, turning, so to speak, my back on that station. In that way only it seemed to me I could keep my hold on the redeeming facts of life." A few pages later, he says that he doesn't like to work, "but I like what is in work—the chance to find yourself. Your own reality—for yourself, not for others—what no other man can ever know. They can only see the mere show, and never can tell what it really means." Finally this: "No, it is impossible to convey the life-sensation of any given epoch of one's existence—that which makes its truth, its meaning—its subtle and penetrating essence. It is impossible. We live, as we dream—alone. . . ."

The theme of Marlow the storyteller is a modernist familiar: ontological alienation, entrapment with no exit, inside the "thick walls of personality." Walter Pater gave us the theory much earlier; Joyce, Woolf, and Eliot the most vivid dramatic images of the artist so enclosed. In Conrad's novella, however, this modernist idea is Marlow's excuse to wash his hands of responsibility. "Work" is an aid to *escape* (which is what he means by "redeem")—escape what is at hand, the realities of imperialist brutality, against which he will not lift a hand. For he is a "worker," "worthy," as his aunt tells him, after he's scorned in her presence the rhetoric of "pity" and "progress," "of his hire."

When reading the patronizing last pages, when Marlow refuses to tell Kurtz's Intended the truth—women are "out of it," he says, they require consoling illusions—we need to remember that it is Kurtz's Intended, at every step, who cues Marlow's responses, leading him to tell her exactly what she wants to hear, she *extracts* consolation from him, even as Kurtz had extracted booty from the Congo, and that it is Marlow's aunt, who is also presumably "out of it," on whom he depends to secure for him his position in Africa. This aunt informs him, when he's on his high moral horse, that he, the worker, is complicitous: utterly "worthy of his hire."

+ + +

There is no document of civilization which is not at the same time a document of barbarism.

WALTER BENJAMIN

Marlow decides that Kurtz is his "choice of nightmares." He means that if he must choose between Kurtz and the Company, which disapproves of Kurtz but only because his "methods" are "unsound," the choice is clear. Like Scorsese's Rupert Pupkin, in *The King of Comedy*, whose goal is also culturally sanctioned, and whose method for achieving it is unsound (but utterly effective), Kurtz is hailed into his extremity by a culture that hypocritically must condemn him for so baldly unveiling its intentions. In extremity, the eloquent Kurtz cuts off, or causes to be cut off, *heads*, and secures them, or causes them to be secured, on the fence posts in his front yard, facing the house. In the name of civilization—progress, pity, and so forth—acts of violence committed against those who stand opposed to European will. As the artist of empire, and the exemplary document of Europe, Kurtz exposes the barbarity of civilization. But not its "criminality"—acts of which are defined and self-interestedly deployed by civilization. The Africans are said to be "criminals," according to the "legality" of the "contracts" that bind them to the Company. At one moment, Marlow calls Kurtz's soul "unlawful." He is wrong: Kurtz and the Company are the law. As Dostoevsky's Raskolnikov would have it, Kurtz is the extraordinary man, the self-defined rightfully violent man. That is to say, the self-defined lawmaker. Under normal grammatical conditions, as opposed to the conditions of Unabomber grammar, it is not possible to say that "civilization" is "criminal."

Has Conrad managed to become a destroyer, inside the racist culture of imperialism? Has he written a new, antithetical word? Or does *Heart of Darkness* demonstrate just how hard it is not to be a voice of the imperial order of things? In the narrative structure of the work, both "Conrad," the frame narrator, who is one of Marlow's listeners on board the sailboat, and Marlow himself seem fascinated and appalled in equal measures. In the final sentence of the book, "Conrad" sees the Thames as a "waterway" rather than a river, a path of imperial incursion, the course of "light," leading always to the outside of Europe—in the last words of *Heart of Darkness*, "into the heart of an immense darkness."

Nevertheless, it is Joseph Conrad-without-quotes, who is not a member of Marlow's audience, not a character inside the tale, but the man who has put this fiction together, the Aristotelean final teller and cause of all narration, who permits the interpretation that neither "Conrad" nor Marlow can have—that every document of civilization is always at the same time a document of barbarism. The thorough-going pessimism of Conrad-without-quotes is to leave us with the conclusion that the choices are inevitably among nightmares, that every place is a heart of darkness, that barbarism is necessarily internal to civilization, those of

Africa and Great Britain alike. In the opening pages, "Conrad" presents London as a monstrosity, the site of essential gloom. In other words, the imperialism represented in *Heart of Darkness* is only the civilized expression of the savagery that underlies the human condition—the rapaciousness inherent in all cultures. Where there are humans, there is order; where there is order, there is violence done to those who stand outside the order: this is the argument of Conrad's book. The antithesis of civility and savagery is false—Kurtz is the link, the embarrassing evidence, and Joseph Conrad is without hope.

Which is to say: Conrad-without-quotes tells us, in effect, that it is not possible to think and write outside the insatiable mouth of imperialism—"insatiable" because its values are materialist—and that, in the end, he is, this antimaterialist, however unhappy with the state of things, a writer who cannot help but be a voice of the dominant culture, not its transgressive undoer, however much he may have wanted to be. Conrad and "Conrad" merge into a single figure, who's been invited, like Marlow, for a pleasant late afternoon's cruise, by his friend and host: the Director of Companies. To tell a story that will ultimately gratify the host: a so-called inconclusive tale of imperialism, full of ambivalences, like a modernist poem, that cannot conclude against imperialism, cannot conclude against anything, is therefore, by default, acquiescent with what it desires to violate, because the desire to violate is unrealizable.

It's hard to cross the line. There is no territory to light out for. Not in Conrad.

+ + +

I killed myself, not the old crone!

CRIME AND PUNISHMENT

When you use the camera as a weapon, you become an informer. . . . There are criminal informers.

JEAN-LUC GODARD

I'm a gangster. If I want something I'll grab it.

JOHN CASSAVETES

John Cassavetes made films, he said, to learn something about himself that he didn't already know. What does he learn by making *The Killing of a Chinese Bookie*? The matchless Ben Gazzara is Cosmo Vitelli—the auteur as club owner, who chooses, directs, and arranges the numbers in his nightly show. "Cosmo": a sophisticate without the endowments of high culture—a rough-edged and poignant Italian-American man of the world, via a very tough neighborhood, who would nevertheless make art. If the audience doesn't like the show, he'll throw them out on their asses. Business is slow. In an early scene, Cosmo, "shylocked up to here," makes his final payment to the loan shark, played by Al Ruban, Cassavetes's real-life producer, who taunts him, "Now you can go out and work for yourself." Cosmo curses the shylock that he has no style, the aesthetic value Cosmo esteems above all else. Style, not class, is what's important. Knocking back highballs in a bar and cruising to his doom in a limo in the hot light of an L.A. afternoon, he claims ironically that he has the world by the balls, that he is amazing—claims that ring hollowly even to his own ears. The three strippers who accompany him on his celebratory gambling venture at the Santa Monica Seven's casino—a rigidly bureaucratic, corporate institution of harsh, clinical whiteness—feel abused by the eyes of the gamblers staring at their tits and asses, something they never have to complain about at Cosmo's highly aestheticized strip club. When he loses $23,000, he protests that he puts all the money he makes back into the club and signs forms 223 and 17. In the sun of the early morning on the way back, his stripper girlfriend expresses concern about what they're going to do, and he blows her off: "It's all paper."

Though he thinks he should get some money and go back to the casino, he instead retreats into the artificial light, the saturated color, of the club to audition a waitress for the show. The club is where he lives, the club is what matters, not life and death, and we know those gangsters can kill him. His girlfriend, who can't tell the difference between art and life, starts a catfight after she sees the waitress jumping around the stage half-naked. Cosmo insists: "I'm a club-owner. I deal in girls." Mr. Sophistication, Cosmo's alter ego and the *raissoneur* of the show, pays tongue-in-cheek homage to French porn in the Paris number, an oblique reference to Cassavetes's cinematic cousin with a shared interest in candid realism, Jean-Luc Godard. As Mr. Sophistication, variously Mr. Fascination, sings "I Can't Give You Anything but Love," Cassavetes hovers in close-up on Cosmo at the bar. Cosmo is Cassavetes, love is the deep subject of Cassavetes's cinema, and love of art in particular is the subject of *The Killing of a Chinese Bookie.*

The Seven, with their ever-present accountant in tow, show up with a problem: a "punk" they can't get rid of. They want Cosmo to kill a Chinese bookie. Surely, a bookie belongs to the same class of louse as a pawnbroker, the victim of Raskolnikov's ideological murder in Dostoevsky's *Crime and Punishment.* And Cosmo and Raskolnikov alike kill for a higher purpose. The gangsters try to connect killing the "Oriental" in this instance with Cosmo's war experience in Korea. His excuses for why he won't do it are multiple: his tough childhood; his desire not to get involved; " . . . you've got the wrong guy. I may be dumb, but I'm not a fool." "I'm a club owner. I took a place from nothing and made it into something," though he doesn't have the figures for how much money the club makes because money holds no interest for him, except insofar as it furthers his art, the purpose of which is to provide the joy of transport. Flo, the muscle of the Seven, persists that Cosmo owes them money and must pay. So they concur he will reduce the debt, but not get rid of it, by taking beautiful girls to Chinatown and inviting the bookie to his club, where he'll be assassinated.

Chinatown, post-Polanski, is a dangerous place of lawlessness, gratuitous death, lack of control. Cosmo complains of the heat, can't eat the food, and escapes where else but into a movie theater, the ultimate sanctuary for an artist, where he loses all track of time and has to rush the girls back to perform at the club—all hell breaking loose there in his absence. Teddy is singing "After the Ball Is Over" and no one is stripping. Before Cosmo can recover the flop, he confesses to Mafia Mort that he didn't want to find the bookie, that he doesn't want to reduce the debt, he simply wants to pay it back. Compromise would corrupt the purity of his artistic endeavor. Whereupon, the long-faced, avenging Flo takes him into an alley and beats the crap out of him, a language that he all too willingly understands. Instead of a ball of string from Ariadne, he gets a .38 army issue from Flo, a map to Chinatown (the labyrinth), and a key to the bookie/Minotaur's home with strict instructions to drive a stolen car there and take a cab back. He must feed the bookie's Cerberus hamburgers in order to pacify him upon his entry. In the oppressive darkness of the car, where Cosmo's face is barely distinguishable from the gangsters', he receives his absurdly strict instructions: no buns, no mustard, no catsup, no piccalilli, no onions. For committing the sin of owing money, the worst sin in the world according to Flo, Cosmo has to forget about art, forget about fixing the show, and commit murder. In the car, sandwiched between the hoodlums and their accountant, Cosmo looks trapped. When the boss gives him the markers to tear up to dissolve the debt, he seals the deal.

En route to Chinatown, the car blows a tire in the middle of the freeway and Cosmo, still a good citizen, runs back to put the hood up. He calls a cab from a payphone, giving his name as Ted (Mr. Sophistication's name). Then he calls the club to find out what's happening on stage, but no one can tell him. On his way to commit murder his primary concern is with what's on stage. He's reduced to singing an irritated rendition of "I Can't Give You Anything but Love" to Vince to try to get him to identify the number on stage, but it's painfully clear that without him his art will die. Just as the death of the pawnbroker at Raskolnikov's hand should mean (as Raskolnikov believes) greater good for others, Cosmo will sacrifice the bookie for the sake of his art.

The Chinese bookie, like Raskolnikov's pawnbroker, is supposed to be alone, but he's there with his lover frolicking in a swimming pool. Cassavetes presents the bookie in his deepest humanity, a naked, wizened old man with his glasses off playfully kissing his girlfriend. Cosmo takes his time, weighing the implications before the shooting. The bookie, blind without his glasses and whistling blithely before his imminent demise, looks at Cosmo, thinks he sees him, shakes his head at the impossibility, then says he is sorry. Coolly implacable, Cosmo kills the bookie, shoots his guards, and jumps a bus then a taxi out of hell. Murder makes him feel like a movie. He stops at a movie theater but doesn't go in. Art can no longer transport him on a trip or a dream out of L.A., out of the United States, where the Almighty Dollar reigns supremely. Movies can't help him now. Frightened, he goes to see his girlfriend's mother, "the best mommy in the world." As he enters, he discovers he's been wounded in the upper right abdomen, the liver. (Cassavetes died of cirrhosis, possibly the result of hepatitis, a metaphorical bullet, contracted while doing a Hollywood movie in Mexico.)

The persistent image in the film is that of a labyrinth: mazes of white or dark corridors and rooms at the club, the casino, the bookie's house, the abandoned garage, where Flo—comically, incorrectly, but with great pathos—informs Cosmo that Karl Marx was wrong when he said that "opium" was the "religion" of the masses (through his teeth): "It's money, money, money." Flo, transformed by Cosmo's capacity for listening, refuses to kill his new friend. Instead, Cosmo kills Mort when the gangsters come after him for the crime of surviving the killing. When Phil tries to trap him, slamming door after door, talking about how it's time to make a deal, Cosmo waits in the shadows, on his way to becoming a shade, then disappears down a stairwell.

Cosmo returns to his "Mommy," but she throws him out because he's a criminal, and he loses the love of her daughter. Back at the club after surviving the hit on him, he finds the crowd unruly, the stage abandoned, and all the artists upstairs in a depression. Mr. Sophistication complains that he, like Cassavetes, has a unique kind of personality, considered "freakish" by some (critic Richard Combs actually called *The Killing of a Chinese Bookie* freakish), that when things go badly he gets the blame, but when things go well the strippers get the credit; there are too many jokes.

Cassavetes's life was like a Cassavetes movie. Described as volatile, enthusiastic, talkative, this intuitive aesthetician of the spontaneous refused to plan because "nothing that you plan will ever come to life." Unlike Joseph Conrad, who in *Heart of Darkness* was dogged by ambivalence toward the rules of the dominant culture, Cassavetes believed there were no rules—"it was up to you to create the language." He hated entertainment and the need within the Hollywood system for artists to bow to studio departmental heads. He thought freely and for himself, directed actors who did the same, and sought out audiences who wanted to take a new step, the very thing Raskolnikov claimed people were most afraid of. After the whirlwind success of his first feature *Shadows,* he worked briefly inside the Hollywood system but the lack of control over his work and the interference were intolerable. Stanley Kramer, in this instance the Hollywood version of Conrad's Director of Companies—and producer of Cassavetes's *A Child is Waiting*—sentenced him to a mere two weeks to edit the film, an impossibility for an artist like Cassavetes, then sentimentalized his work in the final edit. A professional actor who routinely played psychopathic killers, he used his earnings to pay for his "amateur" filmmaking and refused to allow his new thought to be intimidated by his own ego or the businessman's great sums of money.

Just as Joseph von Sternberg said of Dietrich, "I am Dietrich," Cassavetes could have said of Gena Rowlands, his wife, "I am Rowlands." Cassavetes and Rowlands sought an uncomfortably direct intimacy with their audience. When he heard that the preview audience of *Opening Night* cheered when the picture was over, he went back and reedited the last half hour. Cheering was not the feeling he had wanted to leave them with. One of his producers, Sam Shaw, described his work: "John doesn't like perfect shots . . . if it looks too good, he'll change it—stick a shoulder in front of the camera." In his screenplays, Shaw continued, "anything that explains, he takes it out. He's interested in fragments."

With an unerring sense of the presence of truth, in all his films after the improvised *Shadows*, he deftly created a highly structured illusion of spontaneity, the texture of actual life. "To tell the truth as you see it, incidentally, is not necessarily the truth. To tell the truth as someone else sees it is, to me, much more important and enlightening." As Cosmo says to his performers in his final pep talk, "Your truth is my falsehood. Your falsehood is my truth." Cassavetes didn't impose his own truth on the actor's interpretation of his scripts: instead he urged their deepest, most original expression. That insistence preserved the sense of improvisation even in the face of finished scripts.

The Killing of a Chinese Bookie is an allegory of what Ezra Pound called the "serious artist" in America: the artist hopelessly beset by the corrupting demands of the commercial institutions that drive society after the Industrial Revolution. The Mob with its ever-present accountant; the Mob (as Mario Puzo taught us) as metaphor for Business, for which there is only money, money, money and the murder that will be done for money's sake, not, as Cosmo hopes, for art's sake. Business against the Artist, whose sole value is ideal: "Imagination," a key number in Cosmo's club, is funny; it makes, in subjective space, but only there, a cloudy day sunny. Imagination as transformation and transport: values that define Cosmo's desires for happiness, for himself and for those who come to his club. Because Cosmo loves only imagination, he loves and nourishes the club, imagination's local grungy habitat. But Cosmo lives in the world, whose heart belongs to Business, finds himself compromised by contact with the world, must nevertheless deal with the world in order to keep his space of imagination, Crazy Horse West, viable: inevitable dealing that will inevitably destroy him. Cassavetes in this film creates a sensuous lowlife texture, far removed from the abstractions routinely trafficked in by theoretical critics of capital. But beneath that texture, and supporting it, there's an allegorical structure of opposing ideas, of good and evil, that poets from Wordsworth to Yeats, Pound, and Stevens would find congenial: an allegorical structure implying a classic modernist narrative of the end of serious art.

The Killing of a Chinese Bookie was reviled in the *New York Times* by Judith Crist as "a mess, as sloppy in concept as it is in execution, as pointless in thesis as it is in concept." Crist accurately read the film as a kind of remake of "one of those taut little low-budget crime thrillers in which Cassavetes established himself as an actor of noteworthy intensity in the fifties," but she missed the point that *The Killing of a Chinese Bookie* is an autobiographical reinvention of those "taut little low-budget crime thrillers." Just as Cassavetes had to act in those movies, the aesthetic equivalent of murder, to pay for his art, Cosmo has to do actual murder to keep his club alive. Charles Champlin of the *Los Angeles Times* thought Cassavetes "could not decide whether to make a 'popular' picture in something close to the gangster tradition, or another of his studies of contemporary American society." *Bookie* is neither.

The absence in his films of beautiful photography as a value per se constituted his highly original style: the achievement of naturalness through the technique of seeming no technique. The handheld camera work makes what happens immediate, hyperreal. He wasn't interested in the visual power of the image but, rather, in the emotional force the image could carry. The more naked, the less beautiful, the more forceful. He felt about film the way the novelist in Don DeLillo's *Mao II* does about writing a novel—that anybody can do it. He wanted to move beyond obsession with technique or camera angles. It was a process of stripping away, the "via negativa."

Cassavetes's genius, then, was to put us in touch, seemingly without the mediation of artifice, with the inner life of his protagonists and the people who love them. Put us inside their thoughts and feelings by sacrificing conventional technique and angles to get the feeling on film before it disappeared, creating, in the process, a new form: "All we were there to do was record what they were doing. Much like an interview." This Mr. Sophistication of technique habitually fooled interviewers by disavowing technique. Feeling was to Cassavetes what the word is to Godard. "I'm not really listening to dialogue [during filming]. I'm watching to see if they're communicating something and expressing something." The drama is not in what the actors say but in their behavior, and he's documenting their behavior. Cassavetes's film succeeds because his camera finds out what Cosmo thinks and feels.

Cosmo, an auteur–club owner, becomes a killer of a Chinese bookie, no longer an auteur–club owner. He advises his company what he has discovered, that he's only happy when he can be what people want him to be rather than himself, and that the invention of self takes work. "Choose a personality. . . . We'll make their lives a little happier so they won't have to face themselves. They can pretend to be somebody else. Be happy. Be joyous." The joy lies in the performance of "somebody else." But when, at the end, he introduces a new number by the musical director, Cosmo acknowledges that the auteur has been replaced. Still an aesthete of the streets, he introduces the bartender Sonny Venice, savoring the beauty of his name. There will be no more trips of the imagination to foreign lands but only into the interior. Clutching his side as he leaves the stage, he steps out onto Sunset Boulevard, takes his hand out of his pocket and wipes his bright red, bloody fingers all over his dark blue sport coat, strangely comfortable with his new role: that of a man about to die, half in love with easeful death. The final stage image is Mr. Sophistication's weary annoyance when one of the strippers sets a joke fire on his shoulder, another skirmish in the eternal war between art and entertainment, one that causes Mr. Sophistication to leave the stage with distaste.

For Godard, cinema is an act of war. What Cassavetes learns about himself by making *The Killing of a Chinese Bookie* is that the serious artist dies a casualty of the war for art, a victim of the crimes he is forced by a commercial society to commit in order to keep his art alive. Like Raskolnikov, the serious artist kills himself, not the Chinese bookie. In the techniques he deploys, Cassavetes violates Hollywood's rules of the game, succeeds in making a marginal film, but in the tale that he tells, artistic transgression does not touch the imperative of Business. Death, not art, will grant Cosmo deliverance from the American labyrinth—the grip of capital.

+ + +

Almost before he was out of high school he had a name.

DEATH IN VENICE

At fifty, Gustave Aschenbach, Thomas Mann's ironically projected intimate—alter ego, writer-hero—is elevated to the status of nobility. He's now *von* Aschenbach, and all the dead male forebears—the officers, the judges, the departmental functionaries—those who had conducted conscientious, decent, and sparing lives in the service of king and state—all applaud from the grave, having been, at last, duly honored. They now rest, with one exception, who's still agitated, because he's unhappy with the newly elevated, first noble in the family: a restless corpse he is, this maternal grandfather, this Bohemian musical conductor who thinks through his blood. As a man of ardent, obscure impulse, he awaits the day when that so-called distinguished and politically acceptable grandchild of his will become *his* kind of artist—one opposed to the celebrated literary figure, as darkness is opposed to the light. *His* transgressive artist of darkness, not Germany's cultural voice, of international renown, author of the lucid epic on the life of Frederick the Great. Not the careful, so careful weaver of patterned tapestries, that closed fist of a writer, of a man. Not the teacher of a whole generation, whose works are adopted in the schools as models of right prose for the impressionable young—this writer who teaches that modern, psychology-ridden man can still be capable of moral resolution. Not the creator out of duty, in the theater of a rigid, cold service—a balanced artist, admired alike by the general public and the connoisseurs: no, not *von* Aschenbach, but a writer who would violate the culture that honored him, violate and subvert all that he'd hitherto represented. Von Aschenbach, in the growing fatigue of his artistic labors, so publicly pitched, who'd recently become overwrought with his nerve-taxing work; who more and more slept badly—this (joyless) master of fiction would suddenly break loose—lurch toward the scandalously, the destructively subcerebral.

He will cease to submit himself to cold showers before sitting down to his desk; will no more light candles in silver holders and place them at the head of his manuscript, prior to the daily sacrifice. This long dying, Saint Sebastian of the novel—with a wife dead in her youth, a married daughter but no son—can produce sentences now only by prodigious spasms of will. His work is giving more and more evidence of an official tone, a note almost expository—conservative, formal, even formulated—when, one fine day, his writing suddenly and hopelessly blocked, he goes for a long walk in Munich's countryside and sees a redheaded man of gross and somehow obscene aspect and feels, this von Aschenbach, feels the inner barriers open. He envisions a tropical marshland beneath a reeking sky, rank with vegetation—fat, swollen, thick with incredible bloom—and in the heart of it all, a crouching tiger who will devour him, and he feels his heart throb with fear and inexplicable longing.

To Venice he'll go—*his* African Jungle, *his* heart of darkness—to find release and forgetfulness of everything that he's forced himself, with those prodigious spasms of will, to become: forget von Aschenbach. To Venice—this writer who fears he'll be overtaken by death before he's written all that he can write but who at the same time cannot abide what he writes; to Venice to complete von Aschenbach's dying, and then the closed fist, in Venice, will open at last and the arms too in an embrace of . . . of what? Venice (with its "lusty," "lulling," "lascivious" art) is Germany's Other, just as Marlow's Africa is England's.

At the Lido, a beautiful boy of fourteen, Tadzio. Smiles; the smile is returned. Stalks the boy, the son he never had, in guilt and disgust and joy for what he would do to and with him, the boy seeming to welcome his ludicrous stalker, leading him on through the diseased alleys of Venice. Utterly drunk, mad, and powerless to tear his head from his beloved's chamber door, and no longer able to see the danger of being caught, he remembers his forebears, those decent, self-controlled men, and wonders what they would have said about him, the degenerate soldier in the war of art, this slave of Eros, so desperate still to keep his dignity in their eyes.

The revered writer, the would-be child molester, learns of Venice's official secret: the Asiatic cholera ravaging tourism's fabulous city—the secret that would protect commercial interests. Criminally complicitous, self-loathing, Aschenbach keeps the secret of state corruption, and implicitly endorses the regime in place, so much the better to keep his Tadzio in the neighborhood of his own festering desire for a new life and a new art—an art of the open fist, of the blood's unreason.

As he gazes, sitting at the beach, on his boy in the surf, thinking (abjectly, absurdly, yet with sacred fire), I love you! Aschenbach imagines that the pale and lovely Summoner out there smiles and beckons him into an immensity of richest expectation. As so often before, he rises to follow. This time, in death.

He belonged to the red-haired type and possessed its milky, freckled skin.

DEATH IN VENICE

Folklore attests to the dishonesty of redheads but idolizes red or yellow hair streaming out like the rays of sun. During the inexorable course of his Death in Venice, Gustave von Aschenbach, criminal hero, sees a series of reds, agents of his contagion and harbingers of his own decay into fevered redness. In Munich, a pilgrim, distinctly not Bavarian but of unspecified origin (we cannot tell whether he comes from within or without the mortuary chapel), strikingly snub-nosed, with a bald Adam's apple—appears in a cemetery where Aschenbach, aristocratically hook-nosed, seeks the open. Soon he will seek the open within the landscape of his own body.

The sight of this grotesque troll, standing over the beasts supposed to be guarding the doors of the chapel, steals Aschenbach's gaze away from beguilement by the mystical meanings of the scriptural texts gilded on the facade. The pilgrim's existence, "heightened and heightening," forces him to a level of reality that he's long repressed, refuses to allow him to find rest in God's house. The promise of Everlasting Light will not materialize for Aschenbach. Instead, the pilgrim's "bold and domineering, even . . . ruthless air" impregnates him through the eyes with a seizure, a psychic twinge unhinging the heretofore safely locked barriers in Aschenbach's breast, causing him to hallucinate a longing to travel—a lust. Aschenbach regards this longing as contagion and turns away from the pilgrim's hostile, animalistic grimace complete with the curled lip of deformity; bared, long, white teeth; naked gums. A creature of self-will and defiance, double furrows in his visage, this colorless-eyed redhead is no sun god but, rather, a guide to hell, the precursor of Aschenbach's reeking, "steaming, monstrous, rank" vision of desire visually projected. Aschenbach forgets him the next minute, like a random sexual contact, but the contamination is already embedded in his mind's eye, turning him into a kind of tree—"rooted to the spot, his eyes on the ground and his hands clasped behind him."

Aboard a steamer bound from Pola to Venice, Aschenbach penetrates the youthful disguise of a loud old man with cheap, false teeth and rouged cheeks, sporting a red cravat—a kind of gash that will reappear on the beloved Tadzio. Seeing red causes Aschenbach to suffer a "dreamlike distortion of perspective," "a floating sensation" alleviated only by opening his eyes. Much to his horror, a group of lively youths actually enjoys the presence of this young-old dandy who pokes them in the ribs. When he's smitten by the youthful Tadzio in Venice, he will feel the same disgust for himself that he feels for this old man. Heretofore he had neglected cosmetics except for his teeth, but near the end of his journey he frequently visits the barber until, made up and dyed, he resembles this ghastly clown—his lips red like overripe strawberries (the food that infects him with cholera) and wearing a red necktie. With Venice in sight of the steamer, the old man appears again, this time disgustingly drunk, his tongue moving suggestively, his eyes leering. Aschenbach loses perspective, becomes dazed. Then again at the Bridge of Sighs, he barely escapes the drooling importunities of this creature. Like a dreamer, he is all the people in his dream, including this grotesque.

As the young old man stood out among his group, so Tadzio stands out among his friends at the Hotel des Bains. The dreamed eyes of the tiger, the beast that can slay Aschenbach, are transformed into the "strange twilit grey eyes" of Tadzio. This boy, yellow ringleted with the red silk breast-knot and imperfect, jagged, bluish teeth, is the beast of myth that will devour Aschenbach. And it's Tadzio's diseased quality, especially, that excites him. Like the other red beasts, the boy's lips curl spasmodically, uncontrollably, in angry disgust—red signifying lack of control, the very crime that will prove fatal for Aschenbach.

Carrottops: all snakes in the grass, in league with the devil himself—the Arch-Transgressor, the first redhead, reveling in fire. These carrottops mark the milestones in his journey down a waterway deep into his own heart of darkness, guiding him to cross the line into debauchery, disease, and death. Redheads, governed by Mars, the god of war, thought to be temperamental, impulsive, overexcitable, short of attention, quick to frustrate, excessively aggressive, adventurous—all the things that Aschenbach is not. His impulsive desire for adventure is the first sign that he's turning red, turning to the irrational.

Posed like the pilgrim with legs crossed and right hand on his hip, the all too willing Tadzio, leaning over the railing at the hotel, tries to surprise his elderly lover with glances. At the very moment that Aschenbach acknowledges his offense against Tadzio, so vile that Tadzio's mother and governess had several times called him away from Aschenbach's neighborhood at the beach, the Neapolitan jester, the final Satanic apparition, makes his appearance. "A great mop of red hair sticking out in front," his tongue playing loosely in his mouth like the young-old man's, a strikingly large and naked-looking male-defining Adam's apple (like genitalia), the snub-nose and deep furrows of the pilgrim—the horrifying culmination of all the figures who preceded him. This vice-ridden singer with strong teeth (the more bestial, the better the teeth), stinks of carbolic to fend off the plague that, in complicity with the hotel staff, he denies even exists. The guffaws of his song, the stench, the presence of Tadzio paralyze Aschenbach, who watches his life vortex like the rust-red sands in his boyhood hourglass. At his exit, the jester casts off his mask, sticks out his tongue at the guests, and disappears in the night, leaving Aschenbach alone with his no longer sparkling, ruby-red pomegranate juice.

> True, what he felt was no more than a longing to travel; yet coming upon him with such a suddenness and passion as to resemble a seizure, almost a hallucination.
>
> ***DEATH IN VENICE***

The vision of the pilgrim catapults Aschenbach into a landscape, transforms him into a kind of tree in a world of anthropomorphized trees: hairy and misshapen, dropping their naked roots into earth or water (not the cerebral air so long familiar to Aschenbach) as if to suck on huge white breast-like blossoms floating there. And semihuman birds with high shoulders and "curious bills" (a variation on snub-nosed, perhaps). And the eyes of the tiger that excite him to the proper pitch of terror and longing, the zone from within which he would create a new literature, abandoning home, reason, self-control, order, effort.

Fiercely committed to keeping the city's and his own illicit secret, and scorning his classical art and morality in favor of chaos, Aschenbach dreams, late in the novella, when he's far gone, a thing in the theater of his soul. His body is like a country raped and pillaged by some invading Hun, left in ruin. Dramatic tensions dominate his spiritual theater: fear versus desire and curiosity; cruel versus sweet; will versus surrender. A mad rout of men, women, and boys howl the final syllable of Tadzio's name like an incantation. The dreamer's senses and brain reel with the panting bodies, smell of goats, stench of stagnant water and of filth and disease. Struggling in the grip of these sounds and sensations, his heart throbs in anticipation of the pleasure of surrender. Locked in conflict with the stranger god, Tadzio, he finally surrenders to his lust for him, joining in the Dionysian revels—blinding rage, lust to worship, tearing and eating the goat flesh, sticking each other and licking the blood, thrilling to promiscuity, bestial degradation—falling off the Teutonic mountain of life. Just as Stanley Kowalski in *A Streetcar Named Desire* pulled Stella off those columns and she loved it, "having those colored lights going," this stranger god, this boy demon, Tadzio, tears Aschenbach off his mountain. This dream liberates Aschenbach from caring whether anyone suspects him of his crime. The truth of the plague is out now, too. Nevertheless, the dream does not liberate this *von* Aschenbach from his culture's condemnation of his lust; the dream leaves him, in the end, wrapped tightly in disgust, a guilty transgressor. Tadzio has torn him from his mountain, but the Teutonic mountain is inside him.

In *Crime and Punishment,* Svidrigailov, a self-loathing pedophile like Aschenbach, suffers a dream on the eve of his suicide: a cottage full of flowers, housing a coffin of a girl of fourteen, Tadzio's age, who killed herself, because of Svidrigailov's defilement of her, while the wind was howling. The water is rising. In the corridor of the hotel, Svidrigailov finds a five-year-old girl shivering. He picks her up, takes her to his room, undresses her and tucks her in bed. When he checks her, her face turns into the red-lipped, fever-cheeked face of depravity, a whore's face, and Svidrigailov is truly horrified. Knowing there is no saving him from himself—Raskolnikov's sister cannot love him, cannot save him—he finds an official witness for his final performance. At a watchtower, he tells a fireman wearing an Achilles helmet that he is on his way to America, the land where, as he had urged Raskolnikov, it's all right "to go around whacking old crones with whatever comes to hand." Whereupon, he blows his brains out, borne for America, the land that Dostoevsky suggests is the mythical home for criminals, in death or in life.

A camera on a tripod stood at the edge of the water, apparently abandoned; its black cloth snapped in the freshening wind.

DEATH IN VENICE

The key scenes of crisis in Mann's novella—at once meditative and erotic—are staged on the beach, with Aschenbach sitting in a shaded chair, fully clothed, writing gear at hand, watching Tadzio at play in the surf and sand—running, walking, wrestling, or simply standing at the water's edge, especially standing, posed like a work of Greek sculpture: perfect (not human) beauty, godlike serenity, the chaste perfection of Form.

The deepest philosophical issue in *Death in Venice* has been embedded in the Western tradition since Plato and the Neoplatonists. What is the relationship between divinity and the human? The eternal world of

Being (stasis) and the temporal world of Becoming (flow)? The uncontingent Forms of all things phenomenal and the contingent things themselves, the mere copies, the mimetic images of the Forms? Reality and Representation? Reality and Beauty? Can a ravishingly beautiful thing, whether human or of nature or fashioned by the cunning hand of the artist, be a ladder, a bridge, that which mediates divinity? Is it the case, as the erotically interested Socrates tells Phaedrus, that beauty is the sole aspect of the spiritual that we can perceive through the senses? But only a bridge, as Socrates warns, not the Thing in Itself. To linger on the bridge, to love the bridge itself, is to court corruption. To see Tadzio as the chaste perfection of Form, as Greek sculpture, is to see not Tadzio but his idealization in the mode of Greek art. It is to see art, not the flesh.

Aschenbach's meditations on the beach are agonized. Tadzio is "virginally pure and austere," a "young god," emerging from the sea as myth incarnate: the origin of the gods, the birth of Form. But *incarnate:* with dripping locks, a tender young god, an unending delight of the eye, and a delectable feast of the sun. The sun, light source, and divinity's sign of Apollo, showers its wanton splendors on this body, this Tadzio—something in the way he moves: "He ran up, ran dripping wet out of the sea, tossing his curls, and put out his hand, standing with his weight on one leg, resting the other foot on his toes; as he stood there in a posture of suspense the turn of his body was enchanting."

The body of Tadzio, thinks the near-shuddering Aschenbach, was formed of some stuff more "transparent than mere flesh." A transparency through which he gains, thinks he gains, access to divine thought, the single and pure perfection that resides in the mind—not unlike Bill Gray's "pure game of making up" baseball. In Tadzio, an "image and likeness was raised up for adoration." So does the soul of Aschenbach fall from things of the intellect to fix, with intransitive attention, on things of sense, his reason all dazzled and bewitched on a sun-saturated beach. Beautiful things of the senses, that are to serve as memory's tool, in order to set us "afire with pain and longing" for God and our true home, from which we come here trailing clouds of glory, instead entrap us in their fleshly raptures. It is no longer Tadzio as the image *of* that he loves, but Tadzio himself, image in itself, in all of its sensuous particularity, and not image *of*. Aschenbach's relinquishment to the pure image (like a smitten movie-goer) is his corruption, his descent into Plato's idea of hell. As he watches Tadzio romp on the shore, he shivers with ecstasy, feels a seizure to write, and does so, a brief essay on the subject of art and taste. His desire, self-judged as criminal, has catalyzed his writing. At its conclusion, he savors in imagination the taste of Tadzio and feels debauched, he who will never taste Tadzio in the flesh.

Aschenbach's true crime is not one punishable under the legal code, though it would subvert the utilitarian ethos of capitalist culture. His true crime is the assumption of the radical aesthetic attitude, his sinking into sensuous perception, a unique kind of contemplation, conducted not by intellect but *by and for* the senses and for its own sake, without desire for productivity or use. Entranced attention to the image of Tadzio—a pure gaze on the beach before the frenetic and pathetic plunge into pursuit of the boy—is the transgressive act that also subverts the eminently balanced and morally responsible fiction for which his culture had honored him. Entranced attention to the image of Tadzio constitutes a sensuously meditative and musing, rather than an active, homoeroticism: proper spouse of his newfound aestheticism.

From Plato to Mann to DeLillo and Scorsese, the theme is persistent. The image is both corruption and allurement, an absence of Being that we seem, nevertheless, eager to embrace. Mann's Aschenbach, bent on fame from his youngest manhood, dies in the presence of an abandoned camera on a tripod, its black cloth, funeral shroud of authenticity, snapping ominously in the sea wind. Like DeLillo's Bill Gray, Aschenbach dies far from home, trying to escape fame and the unhappy self that he's fashioned inside that fame; dies into the image-worshipping world of the camera that Bill Gray will inherit.

+ + +

Dollars damn me; and the malicious Devil is forever grinning upon me,—and I shall at last be worn out and perish . . . what I feel most moved to write, that is banned, it will not pay. Yet, altogether write the *other* way I cannot. So the product is a final hash, and all my books are botches.

HERMAN MELVILLE, *CORRESPONDENCE*

The moment at which Francis Ford Coppola's *Apocalypse Now* starts to fall apart as a Hollywood film is the moment Coppola and his cinematographer, Vittorio Storaro, begin to achieve Joseph Conrad's aesthetic directive, which defines art as a single-minded attempt to "make you see," to "bring to light the truth, manifold and one, underlying" every aspect of the visible universe, "to find in its forms, in its colours, in its light, in its shadows . . . what of each is fundamental, what is enduring and essential—their one illuminating and convincing quality—the very truth of their existence." Conrad directs the artist in the language of film.

The moment at which Coppola's narrative starts to fall apart occurs after Kilgore, charismatic leader of Coppola's equivalent to Conrad's Eldorado Exploring Expedition (burglars of the Congo lacking moral purpose), has dropped Chief's boat at Charley's point. The mouth of the river, one of the few surfable spots in Vietnam, leads inexorably back in time to Kurtz. Because film is a medium that exists in time, it is antithetical to the spatial art of Conrad's prose, which contains the entire novella in the dense impenetrable jungle of his every sentence. Just as *Heart of Darkness* is a work that must be experienced on the sentence level (much more so than on its narrative level), this is a film that must be experienced on the level of image. The so-called falling apart of *Apocalypse Now* is a function of a catch-22: a film of this length has a habit of insisting on narrative. In effect, Coppola made two films, or one long film in two parts, with the first serving the needs of the culture for plot-driven work and the second serving the needs of the artist for purity of vision. His fear of making the film too long and too slow, together with his financial dependence on the studio, which owned the U.S. distribution rights, forced him to serve two masters, commerce and art. The plot had to fall apart in order for the originality of Coppola's cinematic vision to emerge: the greatness of the film exists not in its plot but in its imagery. Coppola, like Melville before him, fell victim, split in two in his botched attempts to serve these two masters while chasing the ending of the movie, or, in Melville's case, the white whale; the personally troubled later phases of the careers of Melville and Coppola lie, respectively, in the looming shadows of *Moby-Dick* and *Apocalypse Now.*

> Watching the coast as it slips by is like thinking about an enigma.

Storaro shows us the visage of a Vietnam created in the image and likeness of Conrad's imagined Congo: "smiling, frowning, inviting, grand, mean, insipid, or savage, and always mute with an air of whispering." Coppola claimed this was not a film about Vietnam, that it *was* Vietnam. Or is it a dream of Vietnam, white fog like a solid mass dramatizing its impenetrability? It is also the Congo. And finally, it is the American version of what Marlow calls his "work." Marlow, like Willard, his counterpart in Coppola's film, doesn't like his work, but he likes what is in his work: the chance to find himself. Willard's mission is a chance to find himself, which doesn't mean he has to like what he finds. A dark green—almost black—jungle, white surf, the creeping mist, fierce sun. A land glistening and dripping with steam. Conrad's images are all there in the film, and, more important, Storaro renders them in the rhythm of Conrad's sentences. The rhythm of *Apocalypse Now,* after Kilgore drops the boat at Charley's point, realizes in the audience that "state of trance" described by Conrad, an "unnatural" state inhabited even by the trees, "not sleep," but a state in which living things "might have been changed to stone." Those so-called events that do occur: the tiger's attack (green), the sampan mini-My Lai (bright sunlight), the carnivalisque scene at the Do Lung bridge (night with strings of light, flares, smoke, explosions, and a slow strobe effect), Chief's death by spear, the appearance of the photojournalist as commedia Harlequino—all qualify as scenes in what Marlow describes as "a sordid farce acted in front of a sinister back-cloth." They are false and stuffed with sawdust, lit with yellow smoke and played out against a backdrop of burning copters, plastic sheeting, and corpses stuck in trees. Conrad's General Manager, with his starched collars, makes his appearance as the Army General, another hairdresser's dummy, hosting Willard at a roast beef dinner in the middle of a war zone. The Company is still the Company, except this time it's the CIA. The army brass and the CIA in effect perform, in Conrad's scornful phrase, on their "respective tight-ropes for . . . half a crown a tumble."

> You lost your way . . . till you thought yourself bewitched and cut off forever from everything you had known once.

Though the story of Willard and Kurtz is not the tale of Marlow and Kurtz, and the American incursion into Cambodia is not the Belgian burglary of the Congo, the antagonist in both tales is the same: Nature herself, in all her rotting, slimy, writhing force. And though the specifics of the novella and the film are different, the aesthetic vision of the jungle is the same. These visions, in their sheer vivid force, overwhelm the transgressive political desires of both artists. Because what they make us see is so sensuously beautiful, we (like Conrad and Coppola) are seduced away from political arguments against imperialism and war. Nature, both realistically and aesthetically, here defeats abstract idea, political or otherwise. To the extent to which Marlow's/Willard's view from the boat is central to the tale, the true drama is the struggle between Marlow's/Willard's interiority and the anthropomorphized, theatricalized, colorized vision of the landscape. Kurtz is already part of the landscape with the jungle in his heart and as unrestrained as Nature herself. The woods like "the closed doors of a prison" have opened up and taken him inside, and Storaro lights Marlon Brando like a phantom, a shadow, an apparition. He is still, primarily, a voice consumed by darkness. The dramatic question is, Will the landscape also vampirize Willard's heart and mind? Hadn't the doctor in Conrad's novella told Marlow that the changes would take place inside? The tropical landscape is inscribing itself like a creeping disease on his body, the true site of the narrative.

In blue light with red accents, the boat starts to look like a ghost ship floating in blinding fog amid howling arrows. There is a Christo-like red curtain on the bank and purple haze is literally in the air. In their final approach to Kurtz's palace of enchantment, an unreal city of colored smoke and fires, we seem to have ascended to the Hudson River School and achieved the aesthetics of the sublime. The Turneresque images suggest boundlessness, no restraint. Buildings burn in the faces of the men in double exposures and slow dissolves, as the border between interior and exterior turns fluid. The photographs and typescript of Kurtz's dossier end up scattered in the water, dissolving into the eternal river.

The death of Chief follows in great detail Conrad's description of the death of the Black helmsman. When Chief is hit, blood red smoke splashes the background. In the hands of screenwriter Coppola, the Black regular Army Chief, after being shot through the chest with a spear, tries to impale the White CIA lone wolf Willard by pulling his head down on the spear point sticking through his bleeding wound. America just needed a river, a boat, and a jungle as sinister backcloth to play out its particular sordid farce.

Kurtz's logic sounds remarkably like the United States' justification for our presence in Vietnam: "By the simple exercise of our will we can exert a power for good practically unbounded." Marlow's reaction to Kurtz's pamphlet gave him "the notion of an exotic Immensity ruled by an august Benevolence." But like Kurtz, the Americans seemed to have fixated on that "kind of note at the foot of the last page, scrawled" in red: "Exterminate all the brutes." Kurtz, the artist, the criminal, had stepped over the edge. Marlow inhales the atmosphere of the Company, recognizes it as deeply vile, and turns mentally to Kurtz for relief. He chooses his nightmare. Coppola's Willard, on the other hand, fulfills the Company's mission. In killing Kurtz, but not taking his place, Willard, like Marlow, is permitted to draw back his hesitating foot: He does not step over the edge. At the end of the novella, Marlow sits apart, "indistinct and silent, in the pose of a meditating Buddha." In the opening sequence of the novella, "Conrad" describes Marlow as resembling an idol and sitting in the pose of a Buddha, the only one among the group on the yawl who still follows the sea. Or is it the sea that still follows this homeless wanderer, pumping river water through his veins instead of blood. When Willard finally decides to fulfill his mission and kill Kurtz (largely because Kurtz wants him to do it), he emerges from the river with his face camouflaged, like a creature who has lost his human body to a floor of green water, at one with his source at last.

> Going up that river was like travelling back to the earliest beginnings of the world.

Storaro's imagery features the Disneyfication of Southeast Asia and conveys "the dream-sensation"—epitomized in the hallucinatory vision of soldiers surfing in the crossfire. The presence of the past as rendered in a loving mother's letter to her teenage son, Kurtz's dossier, the Dear John letter from Chef's girlfriend—all seem like dreams amid the reality of strangeness. The slowed down stillness is Coppola's version of what Conrad calls "the force brooding over an inscrutable intention." This seeming inaction and sameness watches the actors at their "monkey tricks"—in their reinvention, for example, of My Lai. Conrad said: Make us "see the story . . . that commingling of absurdity, surprise, and bewilderment in a tremor of struggling revolt, the notion of being captured by the incredible." This incredible vision is war imagery aestheticized. Aschenbach's tropical nightmare in *Death in Venice* is not unlike Conrad's dream vision of "trees, trees, millions of trees, massive, immense, running up high." This prehistoric Nature run amok is the proper environment for criminal impulse, the imagery conveying the mysterious stillness of some hidden inner truth, a truth difficult to distinguish from evil. The prehistoric earth of Conrad, Mann, and Coppola is an earth past which these artists glide "like phantoms, wondering and secretly appalled, as sane men would be before an enthusiastic outbreak in the madhouse."

The artist Coppola, at the height of his creative powers, seemingly went mad in the jungles of the Philippines while making the last of his four great movies (*Godfather I* and *II* and *The Conversation* are the others). Kurtz, the criminal artist, didn't make it out alive either, and his legacy is also intact. Inadvertently trapped by Nature and art, forced like Marlow to find himself in his work, Coppola lost himself instead to drugs and women. Or maybe he just didn't like the self he found in the work he thought he loved. Art imitated life so precisely—too much money and too much equipment in the (keyword) *jungle*—that he lost control. So much so that twenty-two years after the original, he reedits the picture with Walter Murch, still chasing Moby-Dick, restoring fifty-three minutes of footage. He no longer cares if the film is too long or too slow. The restoration of the scene wherein Willard visits a French plantation scene is true to Conrad's vision: that this journey is a journey back in time, that imperialism is organic to human history from the Romans to the British, from the French to the Americans. It seems that the greatest artistic offense committed by Coppola, the Kurtz-like emperor of *Apocalypse Now*, was his failure to be true to his vision, and his adherence, instead, to the Hollywood axiom that all scenes must drive the action. He had tried too hard to never get off the boat. Willard and Chef got off the boat to find a mango, found a hungry tiger instead, and the maddened Chef resolved to never get off the boat again. One encounter with a tiger is more than enough. Twenty-two years ago, Coppola clung to Chef's rule: several scenes that took place off the boat never made it to the screen until now. In the end, artistic vision, however flawed, wins out over commerce.

In Conrad's novella, the women at home foster the rhetoric that facilitates imperialism. Marlow's aunt is positively carried off her feet by the humbug idea that justifies the burglary of Africa in the name of enlightenment. Conrad lights the Intended, as Storaro lights Brando in the film: only the forehead smooth and white remains illumined. She controls the story of Kurtz that Marlow will tell her by stopping his words, repeating her own, finishing his sentences to her liking. Conrad's feverishly knitting women, one old and one young, control access to the gates of the Company, the gates of the jungle, the gates of Darkness, of hell itself. The old one wears a look of "swift and indifferent placidity" and glances with "unconcerned wisdom," her face, too, suggesting that of a stone idol. Kurtz's woman in Africa talks like a fury. Far from being out of it, as Marlow insists they are, the women do not stay in their so-called beautiful world. Just as Willard turns to stone, they take in the worst aspects of the world of their men, and the darkness of their hearts. Only their smooth, white foreheads remain illumined in the ever-increasing darkness of the rooms they inhabit. In the making of the film, it is a woman, once again, who plays a crucial role in the course the journey takes. Without Mrs. Coppola and her documentarian's interest in the Montagnards' ritual killing of a water buffalo, Coppola might not have found the particular ending sequence he used in the final version of the film: Willard's killing of Kurtz intercut with the killing of a beast—though the structure of that sequence imitates the intercutting of the baptism ritual with the killing of the heads of the five Mafia families at the end of *Godfather I.*

Though the size of Willard's cranium measures no differently, in the final image the face of a huge stone idol merges into the mask of his face, into the face of his mind, and Kurtz's final words, "The horror! The horror!" repeat in voiceover—his vision not one of grayness without form, like Marlow's. For Marlow, these words constitute a summing up, a judgment. Candor. Revolt. Conviction. Truth. The whisper of the jungle now whispers inside Willard's soul. Willard does not visit Kurtz's Intended or tell the story of Kurtz to the generals and the CIA on yet another journey on yet another waterway. This is one nightmare from which he, like his country, and perhaps like Coppola himself, will never quite wake up.

+ + +

Don't bring your problems to Beirut.

MAO II

Beirut, dead city of the Orient, with its crushed hotels, is the poetic epicenter of the global village. *Mao II* describes Beirut as a place where it doesn't matter if you go the wrong way down a one-way street, as a fantastic dumping ground for the debris of American culture—Hollywood movie posters, signs advertising Coke II—and Oriental memorabilia—ads for Maoist terrorists like Chinese revolutionary posters. Anthony Burgess, in *A Clockwork Orange,* conflated English and Russian culture and language into a terrifying, futuristic vision of casually violent youth. DeLillo collapses American and Oriental, Chinese and Lebanese, worlds into a violent reality, in which "our only language is Beirut." The Maoist terrorist leader in DeLillo's novel is a master of the American mania for celebrity, as well as the Chinese model for the cult of personality, Chairman Mao. This terrorist's vision, both anti-European and anti-Islamic, hovering close to the Korean Sun Yung Moon's, would put Bill Gray into a locked room so he doesn't have to look at him, doesn't have to be reminded of how he "tried to mimic the West . . . put up the pretense, the terrible veneer," the evidence of which has exploded all around him. Like a writer, this Oriental invents history from his filthy room by talking to children, turning them into calm murderers.

Raskolnikov, a not so calm murderer, in a filthy room, wrote an article out of desire to be like Napoleon, who forgot an entire army in Egypt, the ultimate gesture of an extraordinary Orientalist. Napoleon, pyramids, a pawnbroker—a logical progression, for someone dangerously ill. Raskolnikov tells the police investigator that he celebrates the eternal war between ordinary and extraordinary people until the New Jerusalem, of course.

This biblical vision of the New Jerusalem is of a "holy city . . . coming down from god out of heaven." Brita, Bill Gray's photographer in *Mao II*, imagines she might jump off her Beirut balcony and land among a wedding party passing her hotel in the middle of the night under armed guard. She imagines she'll walk along to heaven with them. To the holy city of God?

The pestilence in Raskolnikov's dream in Siberia comes from the depths of Asia. The mass replication of mad, possessed, murderous creatures resembles the terrorist's children and the Moonies of *Mao II*. In Russian history, the terrible price the country paid for the Oriental Tartar yoke was a legacy of autocracy and serfdom. Protest against serfdom landed Dostoevsky in prison under a death sentence, which was revoked at the last minute in a ghoulish performance of the tsar's good will. According to the typical Western vision of the Orient, the danger and threat, the very demons themselves, come from the East. Jack Henry Abbott is half Chinese. In *The Killing of a Chinese Bookie*, the bookie whom Cosmo Vitelli must assassinate doesn't simply happen to be Chinese. He is the fearsome Other—a powerful warlord in a fortress in Chinatown, the equivalent of another country inside Los Angeles, city of angels—whom the mob cannot control. Only the artist can destroy the Chinese bookie and, by doing so, destroys himself.

Asia is the source of cholera, the deadly plague that is a metaphor for Aschenbach's fatal infection with pedophilia. This exotic—Oriental, sexual, irrational, creative—plague would provide (this is his desire) the heated jumpstart that his famous, but cold, writing sorely lacks. He brought his problems to Venice and devoured the Orient in overripe, red, diseased strawberries. He lusted, and hid his lust, just as the city hid its Asian plague. He felt love, and traveled in death to the New Jerusalem, on the waves of the Adriatic, at the beckoning of his beloved boy. The boy "pointed outward . . . into an immensity of richest expectation." And so Aschenbach followed him, to the Orient.

In Conrad's memorable phrase for the motive of European imperialism ("the fascination of the abomination"), the West, with its "fascination" for what it believes an "abomination" (the East), inevitably brings its problems to Beirut—or, in Coppola's vision, its cultural diseases to Vietnam, America's disastrous Eden.

5. ROUGH TRADE

Turn, then, to the case of two orphaned boys: one a slave, one a foundling—a Public Welfare child; one Black and one Black "who's white or pink, but still Black," neither of whom knew his family. Their costumes brand them as members of the dispossessed, in this case, "oppressed and in revolt against whites." Frederick Douglass's first uniform consisted mostly of that which was not: "no shoes, no stockings, no jacket, no trousers, nothing on but a coarse tow linen shirt reaching only to my knees." Jean Genet identified himself as a convict even when he was free: "black apron, black wool stockings and wooden shoes"—a costume he would later re-create for the title characters in his play *The Maids.* Both boys belonged to a group Genet described in his novel *Our Lady of the Flowers:* "that race of children who are hunted down, wrinkled early, volcanic." Both assumed voices that did not belong to them by birth, and they perfected the language of the oppressors that they at once imitated and reinvented. Genet, the formal playwright; Douglass, not a playwright, who in his key "scenes" (nevertheless) is heavily invested in dramatic presentation, theatricality, and ritualized consciousness of his life as a slave, the story of which, at its most gripping, rises from nonfiction to art. One went on to become an incendiary writer, and spokesman for oppressed people; the other went on to become an incendiary writer, and spokesman for oppressed people.

Language, in the shape of the sonnets of Ronsard, given to him by chance in reform school, seduced Genet. Sartre's secretary described the autodidact Genet's writing: "He wrote as an acrobat walked the high wire, as a daily challenge." To Genet the high wire is a metaphor for "the desperate and dazzling region where the artist operates" for himself alone, in an art that demands rigor and promises solitude and, should he fall, poetic death.

Like Genet, Douglass writes in the high-flown, elegantly beautiful language of his oppressors. So much the better to reach his desired audience. In the opening scene of the *Narrative of the Life of Frederick Douglass: An American Slave,* he describes in highly theatrical terms, with a meticulously detailed attention to gesture and image eminently worthy of his compatriot Genet, his witnessing of a "most terrible spectacle," "a horrible exhibition"—the brutal whipping of his aunt and his subsequent hiding in a closet after "the bloody transaction." This scene is his gateway into what he describes as the hell of slavery, his baptismal fall into her foul embrace. Like a good Brechtian actor who employs restraint in the depiction of his own feelings, he thereby unleashes the full horror at the scene in the minds and hearts of his audience, taking us with him through "the blood-stained gate."

The chief offense for which Master beat Douglass's aunt was her failure to fulfill his desire for her presence—"her noble form" and "graceful proportions." Having caught her in the company of another man, a slave, he first "took her into the kitchen, and stripped her from neck to waist," bade her cross her hands, tied them together, and hung her from a hook in order to whip her. Genet, in his play *The Balcony,* also exposes desire as a central culprit forcing precisely this ritual to repeat between slave and master.

As in the neoclassical plays of Jean Racine, in the allegorical plays of Genet, mythic characters, all governed by their destinies, inhabit worlds of strangeness where ritual, disciplined passions, psychological violence, and poetic thrill hold sway in a discourse employing what Roland Barthes in *On Racine* describes as "the obscurities of language, the syntactical contortions . . . under the massive proportion of intentions." The duo of master and slave in the *Narrative* anticipates the trio of judge, executioner, and thief in *The Balcony.* In Genet's play, various clients of a brothel assume, in ritualized scenes with whores, the roles of powerful figures—Bishop, Judge, and General. The clients of the brothel have no names other than the allegorical function they perform. (In Douglass's *Narrative,* characters' names often function as allegorical signs: Mr. Gore, Mr. Severe, Mr. Freeland.) At the outset of *The Balcony,* only the actual Chief of Police has no imitators, though he dearly desires one so that he, too, can be desired and "haunt the erotic daydreams and . . . become a hero in the mythology of the whorehouse."

We hear from characters inside the brothel that out on the streets real revolutionaries rebel against the real figures of power and succeed in eliminating them. The actual Chief of Police enlists the imitators of the Bishop, Judge, and General inside the brothel to take their places in the world outside, but they would much prefer to stay inside and remain imitators. The leader of the revolution arrives at the brothel to fulfill his inevitable role as the very first imitator of the Chief of Police (in Genet's world, as in the real world, revolutionaries must imitate their oppressors), and in a grand gesture castrates himself. Genet explains: "My point of departure was situated in Spain, in Franco's Spain, and the revolutionary who castrates himself was all those Republicans when they had admitted their defeat." The castrated revolutionary dies; the real Chief of Police takes the place of his castrated imitator; the revolution begins again.

Scene 2 of *The Balcony* resembles the scene in Douglass's autobiography: A young and beautiful Thief, played by a whore, *seemingly* chained with bound wrists, her breasts visible, holds out her foot to a larger than life Judge, played by a banker, crawling toward her on his stomach. The Executioner, played by a pimp, stands before her. They reenact the eroticized spectacle of a trial: the Executioner whips and flagellates, the Thief screams, and the banker crawls. Genet accords the Thief the power to burst, should she choose to do so, the Judge's role by refusing to be a thief.

The Judge, paradoxically, says *that* refusal would be criminal. The true crime, according to Genet's grim wit, is to refuse to play your role in the eternal dialectic. The Thief exploits the Judge's vulnerability—makes him crawl—but stops short of refusing to be a thief.

In Douglass's scene of initiation into the hell of slavery—the beating of his aunt—Master is a combination of Judge and Executioner who shares the Judge's erotic desire for the girl's screaming. But when do we get to see Master crawl? The boy Douglass feels terror and horror at the scene and senses unerringly that soon it will be his turn to take part in it.

It was in Baltimore, a second gateway, this time to freedom, that Douglass at the age of twelve began to learn to read and write, skills indispensable to an artist who would be a writer. In Baltimore, his mistress commits a great evil—a crime demanding severe punishment for both Whites and Blacks—in teaching him, an offense that is soon put to right by her husband. Master tells his wife that the ability to read would render the young Douglass unmanageable and worthless as a slave, and make him "discontented and unhappy." These decisive words on literacy awake the giant sleeping in Douglass's heart, the spirit that would resolve to fight, and set him thinking in an entirely new direction. Previously, he had not understood the dark mystery of the White man's power to enslave the Black man, but now Master himself unwittingly lights the pathway from slavery to freedom, proving himself (ironically) a far better teacher than his wife.

The dispossessed hungry White boys in the street take up where the mistress leaves off: Douglass trades bread for lessons. Reading brings him abhorrence of his enslavers, regret for his existence, and a desire for death: it gives him a point of view on his condition but no solution; it gives him the curse and gift of thinking—morbid self-consciousness; and it torments his senses with freedom. The word *abolition* breathes life into him, and prompted by the advice of a good Irishman, a colonial slave, he anticipates escape, which requires not only the ability to read but also to write, for he must write his own pass. After his escape, he gives to a White man who had proven worthy of the title "abolitionist" the privilege of choosing a name for him, with the proviso that he not take away the one his mother had given him: Frederick. The abolitionist, another believer in the force of literature, had been reading Sir Walter Scott's *The Lady of the Lake:* he suggests "Douglass," whereupon a new and enduring identity is born—of a slave, political radical, and epic hero, the noble and unjustly exiled Scottish sovereign.

He learns to write in the shipyard, the place of work where he slaved, by copying four letters from pieces of timber marked for use by the ship's carpenters. Writing for Douglass, in its primal scene, is not for representation of the world but a tool for work that would engage and eventually change the world. In a perfect metaphor of transport, his building of ships combines with his learning to write in order to construct the vessel he would sail out of slavery to freedom, away from the thieving pirate Masters. Continuing his lessons in contests with the poor White boys in the street, he forges relationships across class lines ordinarily fraught with tension and strife. He copies letters with chalk on fences, walls, and pavement and becomes a subversive within a repressive order, "in the spaces left in Master Thomas's copy-book, copying what he had written. I continued to do this until I could write a hand very similar to that of Master Thomas." The student eventually becomes a teacher who commits the unpardonable offense of teaching his fellow slaves to read. He writes himself a pass in the hand of his Master to escape to freedom, where he will use his tool of original language to do the work of liberation.

+ + +

Even when he had the money to pay for them, Genet stole books and told a judge he would be proud if someone stole his books. Cocteau once said of him that he was a great writer but a terrible thief. The very young Genet quickly understood that "everything in life was blocked to me. . . . So I put myself in a position not to become an accountant, not to become a writer . . . but to observe the world. I created in myself, at the age of thirteen or fifteen . . . the writer that I would become." He pointedly spoke French (Parisian) and not the local patois. Fortunate to live next door to the school, Genet visited the teacher there who taught him how to read and write, and he read voluminously, stole school supplies, and, ever the agitator, pushed other welfare children to steal. The orphan played the role of son, knowing this role was merely an illusion, but the role of thief was one he could embrace and own.

Welfare children were not educated in advanced courses past the age of thirteen, but the fortunate Genet was sent to trade school, from which he ran away, to learn typography, a kind of copying, something Genet would never do. Treated like a slave after his escape, he was, as Douglass had so often been, subjected to invasive documentation of his body parts and articles of clothing, colonization of the landscape of his own body by the France he detested so vehemently—the seed of his future rebellious efforts to assist other victims of France's imperialist impulse. The criminal's height, nose, mouth, chin, eyes, complexion, and "effeminate look" were duly noted, along with the color of his clothing. Douglass recognized the brutalizing effects of such "narrow" examinations and "indelicate inspections" of men, women, and children alongside horses, sheep, and swine—all equal in rank. The director of the trade school attributed Genet's escape to "dubious mentality, abused by the reading of adventure novels." So it was literature that urged the boy to freedom; just as it was Douglass's reading of *The Columbian Orator*, including a dialogue between master and slave in which the slave convinces the master to emancipate him, that urged him to the same move. The scene in which Mr. Covey tries to tie Douglass up with a rope provides Douglass his opportunity for transformation into a man resolved to fight. If the Slave refuses to be a slave, he deprives the Master of being. But in his refusal, he imitates the master: he becomes the Arm (the Executioner), repels "by force the bloody arm of slavery," and makes Mr. Covey bleed and tremble "like a leaf."

Before Douglass was put out to be broken by Mr. Covey, he met with systematic starvation by his Master—one known as Captain Thomas Auld because he had not earned the reverence of the title of Master. Douglass calls Captain Auld an "adopted" slaveholder because he came into his slaves by marriage. Since Auld was adopted and poor, he is metaphorically an orphan like most of the slaves he held, and could only assume, bad actor that he was with his inherent awkwardness, the "airs, words, and actions" of a born slaveholder. The role of Master demands the capacity to deceive and the will to power, whether by "force, fear, or fraud," and the attitude of the slaves toward the Master directly bears down upon his ability to play his role. Convert not only to slaveholding but also to Methodism, Captain Auld, a powerless deceiver without resource, doomed to be a "copyist of many" and chronically inconsistent object of his slaves' contempt, despaired of Douglass, who would read the New Testament. Despaired of breaking him, so he put him out to be broken by a better imitator, someone cast more to type.

Mr. Covey, a poor farm renter and professor of religion, whose financial security rested on his reputation as a "nigger-breaker" for wealthy slave owners, would play the role of Master. Not born to his role, and a kind of slave himself, of the poor White sort, he is certainly a better actor than Master Thomas. Covey, the coiled up snake, devoted his life to "planning and perpetrating the grossest deceptions": he was utterly false. If slaves "seemed to think the greatness of their masters was transferable to themselves," Douglass could not have risen one iota in his own estimation through his attachment to Covey, who succeeds in breaking Douglass and, thereby, presumably makes him a slave. But Douglass refused to play the role—refused to "stand, listen, and tremble." After he tried and failed to seek redress from his Master for Covey's violence, he committed the crime of raising his hand against a White man in self-defense. With this act, he made himself a man, and Covey could not complain, because if word had gotten out that a sixteen-year-old slave had drawn his blood, his reputation as a "nigger-breaker" would have been destroyed. Douglass "got hold" of Covey the imitator, and the gesture resurrected him gloriously "from the tomb of slavery to the heaven of freedom."

Because he inhabits what Genet calls "that region of exact freedom" (he means absolute freedom), the Master, like the Judge, is dead: he has ingested what Douglass calls "the fatal poison of irresponsible power." In Genet's world, each judgment, each beating, costs the Master his life: Master's humanity is poisoned by the actions of the role he plays. Douglass, the Christian, feels pity for the slave owner whose humanity is destroyed by his role, while Genet, the radical egalitarian, the unconventional believer who conflated criminals and saints, will recognize only the humanity of his fellow criminals and the dispossessed. Anyone, thinks

Genet, who occupies the upper rung of the power structure is an actor whose gestures are fake. Only those who own nothing and those who subvert all rule and order can lay claim to their own humanity, a humanity, nevertheless, constantly befouled by their desire to play ruling-class roles. To the sublime functionaries who in putting on their robes become corpselike, Genet grants no humanity, but since the leader of the revolution must inevitably imitate his oppressor, he, too, must become corpselike. Douglass, after using his arm against the master (Covey) who would beat him, resolves that though still a slave in form, he could not be one in fact. Once free he will use his arm to write, cease imitation of his oppressors, and escape the deadly and deadening dialectic of master and slave, judge and thief. In taking on the role of artist, he sends his image forth "to haunt men's minds." He lives.

+ + +

> Then there is another kind of artistic work, essentially violent and inflammatory . . . artistic work cannot serve the revolution, and I claim that it rejects all values and all authority. . . . It is the duty of the revolution to encourage its adversaries: works of art. This is because artistic work, which is the product of a struggle of the artist in isolation, tends to contemplation, which, in the long run, may turn into the destruction of all values, bourgeois or otherwise, and their replacement by something that will more and more come to resemble what we call freedom.
>
> GENET

In *The Maids,* Genet describes a failed, obsessive attempt by two sisters to murder their much loved and much loathed mistress. At the end of the play, they succeed in killing the idea of her: Claire, the younger of the two sisters, playing the role of Madame, drinks the poisoned tea they had prepared for Madame, and dies, as her older sister, Solange, witnesses their holy resurrection from the tomb of slavery—Madame's "airy corpse." Like Martin Scorsese's Rupert Pupkin who parades as late night TV host Jerry Langford in his basement and commits the crime of kidnapping for the sake of one night on network television, the maids would rather be queens for a day than "schmucks for a lifetime."

It is reading that urges Solange to freedom: crime news feeds her overpowering desire to kill Madame and escape the bondage of servitude. Likewise, when Douglass was a slave, Mistress used to rush at him "with a face made all up of fury," and snatch from him a newspaper, "in a manner that fully revealed her apprehension." As a free man in New Bedford, he took the paper the *Liberator* and read it with indescribable feelings. It fed him, set his soul on fire, thrilled him with never before felt sympathy for those still gripped by slavery, now envisioned like a larger than life character in a play by Genet—in robes "crimsoned with the blood of millions"—and defined by gesture: "feasting itself greedily upon our own flesh."

A profoundly original work of art is always an assault. In attempting to change our sensibility, to alter our vision, it does violence to our habits.

BERNARD FRECHTMAN, GENET'S TRANSLATOR

Madame, larger than life and crimsoned with jewels and exaggeratedly tragic gestures; two maids, two sisters, who love her enough to imitate her, hate her enough to want to kill her. Reading *True Detective* does violence to Claire's habits—makes her "odd" in the eyes of Madame, interferes with her ability to serve Madame with adequate speed, and causes her to conspire to commit a crime: to falsely implicate Monsieur, Madame's lover, by writing fiction, handwritten letters to the police accusing Monsieur of the most idiotic thefts (crimes, perhaps, not unlike Genet's). Claire's writing of such fiction gets Monsieur arrested and promises to point to her own guilt in falsely implicating him, with retribution sure to follow. Claire playing Madame forced her hand to pen the letters that sent her lover to prison—"without mistakes in spelling or syntax, without crossing anything out." In constructing, through perfectly written fiction, the image of "the lover handcuffed and Madame in tears," Claire tries to kill Madame, but succeeds in the opposite: she turns Madame into a saint of beautiful suffering, elevated to glory by virtue of her association with a criminal.

In Madame's absence, in the play's opening scene, Claire plays the role of Madame and Solange the role of Claire in her attempt to kill Madame.

The maid Claire suspects her sister Solange is actually trying to kill *her* through the mask of Madame, because the maids cannot love one another: "Filth . . . doesn't love filth." They cannot love one another because they do not wish to be one another. They can only love and wish to become Madame, whose degrading view of servants they have internalized. Claire, as Madame, must, accordingly, loathe servants: "They're not of the human race. Servants ooze. They're a foul effluvium drifting through our rooms and hallways, seeping into us, entering our mouths, corrupting us. I vomit you!"

Douglass, contrarily, loves his fellow slaves "with a love stronger than anything I have experienced since" and writes the fictional passes for himself and his fellow slaves in their first attempt to escape. In the act of spreading manure, he, like Claire, is overwhelmed with the feeling of betrayal, clearly by one of his beloved, not despised, fellow slaves. Arrested, he burns and others eat their passes, destroying the literary evidence, vowing to "own nothing." Separation from his fellows, which he so desperately dreads, facilitates his subsequent successful attempt at escape.

Once he does escape, for a short, distressing time, he can trust no man: For one to understand his situation, he says in a monologue worthy of Racine, one of Genet's models: "Let him be a fugitive slave in a strange land . . . let him place himself in my situation . . . let him feel that he is pursued by merciless men-hunters . . . let him be placed in this most trying situation . . . then . . . will he fully appreciate the hardships of and know how to sympathize with, the toil-worn and whip-scarred fugitive slave."

After Claire has failed to poison the actual Madame with tea and phenobarbital, Solange refuses to play the role of slave, "to sit here and shake," any longer. Claire determines to drink the tea herself—as Madame. In so doing she successfully separates herself from Solange, who in a completely theatrical gesture rises up free from Madame's "icy form" to join the ranks of the criminal/saints. Solange succeeds in destroying her sister, the imitator of Madame, just as Douglass succeeds in assaulting Mr. Covey, the imitator of Master. The difference is that Douglass, in a register decidedly less fantastical than Genet's and governed by compellingly real circumstances, really does eventually rise up free from Covey's trembling form, and all the slaves, "not they themselves, but rather the hellish agony of their names, are present at his side."

+ + +

> I am going away to the Great House Farm!
> O, yea! O, yea! O!

Slaves selected to do errands at the Great House Farm, who campaigned for these posts like candidates for political office, sang rude and incoherent songs on their way, songs in which rapturous sentiment conflicted with pathetic tone, and pathetic sentiment conflicted with rapturous tone. Rapture and pathos coexisted disharmonically, just as the clanking of fetters and the rattling of chains were readily heard simultaneously with the solemn prayers and pious psalms of the slave owners, whose religion generously provided great cover for great crimes. While still a slave locked in the inexorable dialectic of longing for the great house and despair at his subjugation, Douglass did not understand the meaning of these songs. The songs impressed his consciousness, but it took freedom to make the tears run down his face.

He "sometimes thought that the mere hearing of those songs would do more to impress some minds with the horrible character of slavery, than the reading of whole volumes of philosophy on the subject could do." To those songs he attributes his "first glimmering conception of the dehumanizing character of slavery." Douglass would send anyone who wishes into the wilderness of the deep woods of Colonel Lloyd's plantation to become the sounding board of the slaves' rapture in pathos and pathos in rapture—that their souls, too, might be impressed. Marked by those sounds, they could not, as so many Northerners did, speak of the singing "as evidence of their [slaves'] contentment and happiness." Analysis of the sounds would make them hate slavery and sympathize with those held in its bonds: a fulfillment of Douglass's political intention.

In the landscape of *The Balcony*, the inevitable progression of rebellion is evaporation and metamorphosis into song. A whore, rescued by the leader of the revolution from the brothel, the bastion of illusion, fights for the cause in the political world. But when the revolutionaries need to turn her into a song to revive their flagging efforts, she becomes trapped in illusion again. And when the pimp returns to the brothel from the streets dominated by revolution, he reports that what was most awful, more awful than women urging men to loot and kill, was a girl who was singing. Like Douglass, Genet believed in the power of singing to impress the soul of the listener. The Chief of Police hopes the songs of the rebels will be beautiful because if they are beautiful they will not give the rebels courage or make them willing to die for their songs: beauty and politics are incompatible. For Genet, if the singing is beautiful, it ceases to be a political tool, and if it becomes a flag for a political cause, it ceases to be art.

Genet's last play, *The Screens,* sprawls the depth and expanse of French colonial involvement in Algeria. The major design element of the play, as reflected in the title, signifies the dominant tension between the world of real objects and the world of aesthetic representation, between reality and illusion. First, ever ambivalent about his political and aesthetic impulses, Genet wrote to Roger Blin, the director of the original production, that *The Screens* was "nothing but a long meditation on the Algerian War," then three years later, "Don't bother too much about the Algerian War." The traitorous thief Said, his ugly wife Leila, and his anarchic Mother dwell in the nettles (a reference to Genet's own name) and love with the language of the two maids—the powerful, ugly language of hatred and rage, of those who have been cast off. *The Screens,* among other things, is about criminality: choosing evil as the only real freedom, the only way to postcolonial self-discovery and reinvention.

With each traitorous betrayal of his own people, the colonized Arab population, Said's reputation and "deified abjection" grow. The Arabs rebel against the colonial forces, setting fire to the orchards in a series of drawings of fire on the screens. In this surreal landscape, Master Harold, the French colonist, has a wonderful pigskin glove that flies in like a sculpture of Douglass's bloody arm of slavery to speak with Master Harold's voice and guard his slaves. The French, so absorbed in beauty that they fail to notice the fire, consider themselves a necessary pretext for the revolt of the Arabs against them: "If not for us . . . they'd have gone under."

The mother of the thief and antihero Said trumpets the importance of refusing to serve any purpose whatever, warns her son of the fate he risks: immortalization at the hands of the Arabs in a song. She's in danger of having a village square named after her because of what she considers a "lousy break"—she almost unintentionally strangles a French soldier caught in the straps of his knapsack. Shattered by the prospect that she will be turned into a symbol, this eternal anarchist advises her son: "Squelch the inspiration, shit on them!"

Genet's play traverses the land both of the living and of the dead. When characters die, they break through the paper of the screens into the Underworld. The dead would welcome Said, the "little heap of garbage" that inspires them, their prodigal son who teaches them how to lose themselves, who has gone so far that he's become impossible to judge. They would "embalm" his "shittiness, so that none of it's lost." The living, the Arab Combatants, exit the brothel, for Genet ever the house of illusion, to demand that Said come with them and change his skin from that of a traitor to his people to that of a Combatant like them. (Unlike Said, Genet sided with the Algerian rebels.) When Said tries to run away, they shoot him, but he keeps his identity as the outsider. His wife does not die; she literally disappears, swallowed up by her clothes. Said, too, does not cross over into the world of the dead, nor is he turned into a song. Instead he descends, as only he and his loathed/loved wife know how: they sink into another region of neither the living nor the dead.

I don't want to publish anything about France. I don't want to be an intellectual. If I publish something about France, I'll strike a pose as an intellectual. I am a poet. For me to defend the Panthers and the Palestinians fits in with my function as a poet. If I write about the French question I enter the political field in France—I don't want that.

GENET

By insisting on the ambiguity and apolitical nature of his work, Genet refused to let his plays be turned into songs to serve some political purpose. Despite this insistence, the military, enraged by a scene in *The*

Screens in which French soldiers fart French gas to honor their dying lieutenant, repeatedly stormed the stage during performances—much to Genet's delight. Considering Said/himself a "little heap of garbage" that must be protected from being turned into a flag, Genet, the dedicated anarchist and advocate for the Palestinians, said, "Listen: the day the Palestinians become institutionalized, I will no longer be on their side. The day the Palestinians become a nation like other nations, I will no longer be there. . . . I believe it will be at that moment that I will betray them." Since he subscribes dearly to the theme of *The Balcony,* that the revolutionaries inevitably imitate their oppressors, he argued that the Jews had taken on the inhumanity of their former masters, the Nazis, in their treatment of the Palestinians. For Genet, the moment criminal violation becomes successful it is no longer violation. Authenticity lives only in the act of rebellion, a negative critique without positive alternative. He can only support a revolution in process, not on any so-called success. The thief Said, like the thief-turned-writer Genet, would free himself of cultural colonization: by isolating himself, by refusing to be turned into a song, by revolting into eternity instead of going to heaven.

Genet believed his homosexuality made him "perceive that Algerians were not different from other men." For him, homosexuality was the great leveler of race and class, but he did not write his "books for the liberation of the homosexual. I wrote my books for another reason altogether—out of a taste for words, out of a taste for commas, even punctuation, out of a taste for the sentence." He wrote books out of a taste for aestheticism. Although Genet advocated for the Black Panthers, some Blacks took his homosexuality and the fact that his skin was not black as indicators that he was different from them. The Black writer Ed Bullins insisted that "Black people cannot allow white perversion to enter their communities, even if it rides in on the black [*sic*] of a Panther." Bullins warned against Genet's "faggoty ideas about Black Art, revolution, and people" and the fact that Genet had admitted seeing himself as a "so-called 'nigger.' "

Between 1961 and 1984, Genet wrote nothing substantial but progressed in his role as poet to political advocate standing with the dispossessed of the Third World, the Palestinians in particular, and defending the Black Panthers. If the poet/anarchist would become political, he must stop producing art. Douglass, for his part, "took right hold of the cause" of antislavery reform with the same vigor his former masters had employed in regularly "getting hold" of him—the expression they used to indicate the taking of violent action. Genet and Douglass shared the conviction that thinking and writing are far more dangerous than weapons.

+ + +

I wish I were Black. I want to feel what they feel.

GENET

Or is it, that as in essence whiteness is not so much a color as the visible absence of color, and at the same time the concrete of all colors . . . ?

MOBY-DICK

Though Genet, perennially obsessed with reciprocal power relationships, wanted to be Black, Sartre compared him to Melville's white whale—"formidable and familiar," "white and polished as a sheep's bone"—calling Genet "the Moby Dick of pederasty." Genet, whose work is obsessed with dialectical tension, contains within himself the extremes of Black and White. The whiteness that Melville describes in *Moby-Dick,* and that Sartre, by inference, ascribed to Genet, "enforced a certain nameless terror." An "ungraspable phantom of life"—a demon, sailing in the invisible sphere of the imagination—"a colorless, all-color of atheism from which we shrink," Genet cannot be grasped, captured, contained, or controlled by any structure of power, social or political.

For the Black and White Genet, it's just a short walk on the high wire from the world of *The Maids* to the world of *The Blacks.* The two maids dressed like foundlings, the slaves of Madame, and the characters in *The Blacks* are all figures of myth. Genet's biographer Edmund White thought that the title *Les Negres* "might better be translated as 'The Niggers' "—a title Tennessee Williams regarded as "suicidal." Genet's translator Bernard Frechtmann opted for *The Blacks,* because in 1961 the word *Black* was still considered negative. The subtitle of the play is *A*

Clown Show. The Blacks arrives onstage with a funeral mass for a White woman, not just any White woman, but the mother of the White race, raped and murdered, and the trial of the accused: a Black man named Village, because it is the whole community that is tried for the crime. He must reenact his crime before a court made up of Negroes wearing White masks of colonial figures: Missionary, Judge, Governor, Queen, Valet. And his love of the whore aptly named Virtue testifies further to his Whiteness—his (Douglass-like?) addiction to love instead of the far more useful hatred.

Offstage there is another trial going on: the trial of a Black traitor to a planned uprising by Blacks. He is condemned and executed by an all Black court. The tension prevalent in Genet's work between the real world and the world of aesthetic representation exists here between the fantastic poetic-religious ritual onstage and the real trial and execution offstage. The character Newport News thinks this execution should stop the Blacks from playacting among themselves (though they can put on an act in front of White audiences) and teach them to take responsibility for spilling the blood of their own people. Though the Blacks in the play have achieved freedom, they must free themselves from internalized Whiteness before they can reinvent or discover a culture truly their own, free of colonial influence. The real struggle offstage is both ideologically and spatially peripheral to the ritualized struggle onstage through which the Blacks, who are ruled, still identify with the Whites, who rule.

It is precisely the way in which the theatrical world is overtly signaled as being distinct from the actual world that makes transformation and revolution possible in it, since in Genet's view the real world is not capable of this kind of transformation. Reality is deceitful and inadequate; art and appearance are the only place to look for compensation. Offstage, one traitor is executed and another leader continues the fight. Newport News: "Our aim is not only to corrode and dissolve the idea they'd like us to have of them [the Whites], we must also fight them in their actual persons in their flesh and blood." But in the end the Blacks overcome the Whites only through fantasy as they ritualistically exterminate the members of the White court (Negroes wearing White masks).

This play is not written for Blacks but against Whites.

GENET

On his arrival in New Bedford as a free man, and not hearing any "loud songs," "deep oaths or horrid curses" on the wharves there, Douglass did hear of a meeting, a kind of trial, called under the notice "Business of importance." A colored man had threatened a fugitive slave, with whom he was on "unfriendly terms," that he would inform his master of his whereabouts. The "spirited" colored people, determined to protect each other from a blood-thirsty traitor, invited the traitor to come to the meeting at which they appointed a very religious old gentleman as "president," a kind of judge. First the judge prayed and then he said: "Friends, we have got him here, and I would recommend that you young men just take him outside and kill him." If some "more timid" attendees had not interrupted the majority from "getting hold" of the traitor, the members of this makeshift court, its jurors, would have carried out this prayerful sentence. The betrayer escaped, disappeared, and no more such threats as his were heard thereabouts.

If the traitor in Douglass's *Narrative* had been caught and murdered, Genet—had he been a reader of Douglass—would have approved of this murder transformed into ceremony. But inside the scene of Douglass's "trial" the so-called timid ones—true Christians and true revolutionaries—would break the cycle of imitation of the Whites, who use Christianity as a cover for crime. They would not let their brother, albeit a traitorous one, be killed. Instead, he disappears, leaving the memory of him to haunt any other would-be traitors and to suggest the possibility that the cycle of imitation is not yet eternal.

Archibald: Negroes, if they change toward us, let it not be out of indulgence, but terror.

THE BLACKS

The "president" at Douglass's business meeting would terrorize would-be traitors, but the timid prevent the coloreds' ritual repetition of an earlier scene in the *Narrative* that sent a "thrill of horror" through all who witnessed it: the scene of Mr. Gore's cold-blooded shooting of Demby, the slave who refused to come out of the creek to be whipped. The thrill of horror, the inherited culture of the Whites, persists in the imagination of the free slaves and would drive them to repeat murder but for the original thinking of the timid few who barred the will of the majority. The timid, by being called timid, are censured for their unwillingness to participate in murdering the would-be traitor, but by virtue of their timidity, the souls of many were not stained with their brother's blood. Killing the colored would-be traitor would not have been regarded as a crime just as killing a slave was not regarded as a crime. No sensation would have been produced in the community, no murderers would have been brought to punishment: to the free Blacks this would-be traitor's life was still worth only "a half-cent." The disastrous transformation of the community into the vicious White Master (Mr. Gore) was nearly achieved.

+ + +

They talked the talk and walked the walk of their oppressors—Douglass's marcelled hair, Genet's "impeccable grey suit." Both dandies, both body artists, sensitive to the theatricality of everyday life, who turned their appearances and actions into works of art. Baudelaire would have recognized the spirit of their lives singing of "opposition and revolt: all [dandies] represent what is best about human pride, this need, all too rare among people today, to fight and destroy triviality. Dandyism appears especially in those transitional periods when democracy is not yet all-powerful, when the aristocracy is only beginning to stumble and grow old. In these troubled periods, certain men—declassed, disgusted, out of work but rich in native strength—can come up with the idea of founding a new kind of aristocracy, all the more difficult to break since it will be based on the most precious and indestructible human faculties as well as on heaven-sent gifts that work and money cannot obtain. Dandyism is the last burst of heroism in periods of decadence." The volatile combination of crime and art gave these rebellious dandies, these vagabonds, their status as legends.

Another sort of legend altogether, Lee Harvey Oswald, met with Genet's approval:

Not because I have a particular hatred for President Kennedy; he doesn't interest me at all. But this solitary man who decided to oppose a society as strongly organized as the American society and even as Western society or even as every society in the world that rejects Evil, ah yes, I'd rather be on his side. I sympathize with him, but as I would sympathize with a very great artist who would be alone against all society, neither more nor less, I am with every man alone.

GENET

Genet's alignment with this political assassin exiles him to his island of moral isolation and artistic greatness, even as Douglass ascends the political platform, morally triumphant, to raise his voice against Evil.

6. DELIBERATE ORPHANS

After the rapid-fire commercial and critical debacles of his most ambitious books, *Moby-Dick* and *Pierre,* Herman Melville entered the terminal phase of his long despair and wrote the novella *Bartleby the Scrivener: A Story of Wall Street.* The title character is a copyist in a law office about whom nothing is "known," we are told by Melville's lawyer-narrator, who is also Bartleby's employer, except by way of one vague rumor concerning a past occupation as "subordinate clerk in the Dead Letter Office," Washington D.C. What the narrator has witnessed in the office itself is all that he actually knows, but what he's seen and heard is so teasingly enigmatic that it is difficult to say what, if anything, is "known" in any rigorous sense, so that no reader, starting with Bartleby's first reader, the narrator himself, can respond without succumbing to Melville's hermeneutical tease and quickly moving to the level of allegory and parable—as promptly do we; allegory and parable embodied in the realistically observed details of the nightmare world of middle-class labor—Wordsworth's "savage torpor" migrated to the white-collar zone: Kafka's Melville. *Bartleby the Scrivener* is the story of a kind of writer, a writer in crisis, very like

Melville, who here takes his own career as a representation of the destiny of the serious artist in a hostile environment—hostile meaning commercial: Wall Street as metaphor for Melville's America.

+ + +

Virtually unlettered, at twenty-five Melville had begun with conventional and popular books, *Typee* and *Omoo,* fictions of raw experience filtered through generic imagination—bearing his genial charm, to be sure, but in a sense copies of literary forms already securely in place in American culture. Suddenly a famous author and thinking that he could live as a writer, he discovered the world's great literature, became the most voracious of readers, deserted convention—that is, deserted scrivening—and was inspired to an act of originality—the equivalent, it turned out, of an act of artistic suicide. Consequently, in his third book, *Mardi*—longer even than *Moby-Dick*—he transformed the romance/travel narratives of his popular successes into a demanding (and often tedious) exploration of philosophical and political themes in obscure symbolic terms of voyaging, a meticulous record, in effect, of his own recent voyages in the library. The critics were unhappy; the readership that he'd won with *Typee* and *Omoo* would not buy.

Now married and with a growing family, and doubtfully self-supporting—yet committed, nevertheless, to living and to sustaining his family, by the work of writing—work that his culture would increasingly refuse to recognize as such, would not remunerate, in any event, except on its own, conventionalist terms—he needed to try again to please the culture (and himself, too, somehow) with *Redburn* and *White-Jacket,* which he wrote in less than a year: literary fare reminiscent of *Typee* and *Omoo,* with young male adventurers set traveling in strange new worlds, yet no genial romances were these, with their fixations on sordid and brutal social scenes. The public would not eat; stubborn Melville persisted in what he told Hawthorne were his "botched" ways and poured out *Moby-Dick* and *Pierre:* "Dollars damn me," he wrote to Hawthorne. "What I feel most moved to write, that is banned,—it will not pay. Yet, altogether, write the *other* way, I cannot."

A bare chronology says much of what there is to say about the gargantuan literary energy that was Herman Melville:

1846, *Typee*
1847, *Omoo*
1849, *Mardi*
1850, *Redburn*
1850, *White-Jacket*
1851, *Moby-Dick*
1852, *Pierre*

In the space of seven years, James Joyce wrote *Ulysses.* In the space of seven years, Melville wrote the equivalent of four books the size of *Ulysses,* one of which was *Moby-Dick.* All by his mid-thirties. Then this growing failure of a writer followed with a few stories in the mid 1850s and *The Confidence-Man* in 1857. And then, for the last thirty-four years of his life, no more fiction in public print. On his death in 1891, the *New York Times* ran the obituary of *Henry* Melville. Another New York daily reported the death of *Hiram* Melville. In *Bartleby the Scrivener,* published in 1853, Melville saw his life whole, as it was and as it would be.

+ + +

At the time of Bartleby's advent, Melville's lawyer-narrator is the newly appointed Master of Chancery in New York City—a legal safeguard of wealth founded on the privileges and obligations of private property. As he puts it, he does a "snug business among rich men's bonds and mortgages and title-deeds." And he also describes his law office as a "snug retreat"—as if to say that the legal business of property and the place of business provide him bodily and psychological warmth. He mentions (all of this with some pride, at the beginning of his story, by way of introducing himself to his reader) that he was once employed by John Jacob Astor, whose very name affords him (present tense) aural pleasure: "a name which, I admit, I love to repeat, for it hath a rounded and orbicular sound to it, and rings like unto bullion." For the narrator, the business of property and the names of the fabulously wealthy are a sensuous font of creaturely comfort and even, for this stolid, tightly lidded fellow, erotic lift.

Business for the new Master of Chancery (he's pleased to note) is heavier than ever. Another scrivener is needed, Bartleby answers an advertisement, is hired, and promptly sets to copying with boundless energy day and night, with no breaks for meals. One day, abruptly, for no discernible reason, he begins to announce his gentle but unshakable refusals. The first of his famous I-prefer-not-to's is a refusal to proofread, though he continues to copy sensitive documents with the same formidable energy. When his employer requests that he run a routine errand, he again says, "I prefer not to." Then refuses to do the work of copying. He won't do his job. Then, finally, to vacate the premises: into the heart of Wall Street comes what can only be regarded by a true Wall-Streeter as a strange kind of madness. All along the way, when asked for his reasons, Bartleby only says: "I prefer not to." Our narrator, who prides himself on his prudence and self-composure is, by turns, confused, (undemonstratively) enraged, self-serving, fearful for his sanity, and—most problematically for him—deeply bonded to Bartleby by what he calls "fraternal melancholy."

In a sense, Bartleby's employer and storyteller never advances beyond his initial impression of "a motionless young man [who] one morning stood upon my office threshold, the door being open, for it was summer. I can see the figure now—pallidly neat, pitiably respectful, incurably forlorn." His first impression is reread in the retrospective moment of narrative composition: by telling a story, he would know Bartleby. (This is the tale of two writers.) "Motionless," he says, upon the threshold. Did he expect amazing gyrations? The lawyer's redundant image of Bartleby upon the threshold reconstructs the original moment with what his narrative understanding has been able to distil of Bartleby's deep significance for him. Bartleby, he tells us often, is "cadaverous." What our narrator intuits, as he narrates, is that a dead man had answered his advertisement. The image of "pallid" Bartleby upon the threshold is this storyteller's foreshadowing of Bartleby's actual death at the end of the tale, but also—this the lawyer never quite grasps, it's at best a presentiment at the edge of consciousness—the threat of a larger death, social and economic: death systemic. So a third writer emerges, the reader (ourselves) who would know the unconscious of Melville's narrator. There, on the threshold, says this third storyteller, stands the refusal of the social system founded on private property, a refusal of the lawyer's way of life, to which the lawyer, against all that he values, finds himself mysteriously drawn.

Like Captain Ahab before him, about whose background we are given but one salient fact, that he lost his parents when a year old, Bartleby comes to us as an orphan—of sorts. Unlike Ahab, or Melville's most famous narrator, Ishmael, he's an orphan very like Melville himself, an orphan apparently by desire, with designs on those who would read him. Bartleby presents himself self-shorn of background, parentage, original place—they do not pertain, whether or not he has such rooting. He "had declined," reports the lawyer, "telling who he was, or whence he came, or whether he had any relatives in the world." (In this regard, the lawyer is almost as unforthcoming: he is Bartleby's hefty spectral double, his brother in melancholy and loneliness.) It is as if Bartleby would say, To know me is to know the meaning of irremediable isolation, my "incurable forlornness" and bottomless sorrow. Having, and knowing, one's parents matters not. As if he would say, My orphanhood is not personal but ontological—a communicable disease of being here, in this place, at this time; disease fatal to me and all that I contact.

Melville, who lost his father at twelve, had projected himself as Ishmael, cast into the wilderness. In the course of *Moby-Dick,* Ishmael is drained of his violence, but in the closed economy of that book, violence flows into and becomes Ahab: Antichrist of Will. Bartleby, who is nothing like Ahab, nevertheless shares this with him: both set themselves against powerful American institutions. In his pursuit of metaphysical revenge, like the serious artist who would transgress the order of things, Ahab would undo the whaling industry, hub of the American economy in the first half of the nineteenth century, if that's what it would take to sink his lance fatally into the White Whale. While commerce has no "use" for metaphysicians, just as it had no use for Melville's symbolic art of *Moby-Dick*—a kind of revenge exacted on the scrivening of popular literature—the reverse is not true: both metaphysicians, Ahab and Melville, have much "use" for commerce. Neither the one's quest nor the other's symbolic art is imaginable outside the contexts of business (whaling, conventional fiction) against which Melville and his most memorable character (and most violent self-projection as writer) set themselves. Bartleby—the purer allegorical instance of Melville's idea of the dangerous artist, his most romantic idea of himself—would subvert the country's financial center. His refusal to read proof raises the insurrectionary possibility that error and chaos will rule the relations of private property. In their unalterable indifference to the practical life of getting and spending, Ahab and Bartleby are the loosest of social cannons—transgressive artists in the guise of the orphan without obligation to the social system, the unnourished orphan who owes nothing.

And the stories of both are stories of walls. Wall Street; the towering walls that hem in the building of the Master of Chancery and offer views only of themselves—views that Bartleby is often found enjoying in what the narrator calls a "dead-wall revery"—and the "wall" of the White Whale. In the midst of his initial address to the crew, Ahab asks: "How can the prisoner reach outside except by thrusting through the wall?" Ahab thinks of the totality of natural phenomena as God's—or the Devil's—cunning artifice: the wall of nature, his prison, and nothing more than a "pasteboard mask" through which he would smash to the other side, to the real thing, the Malicious First Artificer who fashioned the wall in its most maddening form, that of the White Whale. But Ahab's titanic will is no instrument of his freedom, is never free will. For all his huge force and power over the crew, he's driven uncontrollably in his pursuit of Moby Dick; doing otherwise is unimaginable, even to himself. Ahab's will, in Melville's conceit, is not his own.

Bartleby's passivity would appear to cast him as the least likely of Melville's characters to embody the role of the free man, but he may in fact be Melville's one free man, his most dangerous creation. On the second occasion of his refusal to proofread:

> "I would prefer not to."
> "You *will* not?"
> "I prefer not."

Bartleby's correction of the lawyer is in effect a rewriting of the vocabulary of freedom: while "prefer" and "will" equally signify choice, Bartleby's "prefer" carries always (spoken or not) the subjunctive mood ("would prefer"), the tense, as it were, of imaginative space. Bartleby implies that he contemplates possibilities before settling on the one that pleases, that his preference is an artist's preference among options, that his choice is truly free choice, whereas the lawyer's "*will* not" suggests Ahabian drivenness—Melville's italics indicating vocal stress, a voice under stress; only one possibility to be chosen, therefore no "possibility," therefore no choice, no freedom.

The comic introduction, before his appearance on the threshold, of Bartleby's coscriveners places his refusals in an allegorical framework. "Turkey" and "Nippers," known only by their nicknames, mutually conferred and deemed (by their employer) expressive of their respective characters, are given to us as complimentary temperaments, mechanical creatures driven by physical causes, who are useless half of the day—one in the morning, the other after noon. At their respective times, these pup pets of the digestive tract are irritable, paroxystic, and (most important) inefficient. But since one is "on" while the other is "off," and since both, when on, are exceptionally "useful"—the narrator means good for business—the day is well covered. "Their fits relieve each other," he says, "like guards." The lawyer is pleased. He hires Bartleby because he thinks that such an addition to his staff will make him even more pleased, because "the appearance of one so sedate" could not but help "operate beneficially" on the two automatons. He means, make them less subjugated to biology, more productive as scriveners. To complete this allegory of bodies: recall Bartleby's exceptional leanness, his anorexic habits. Melville's savage implication is that Bartleby's "freedom" from his body is a function of his refusal to eat. To be free in Wall Street America is to die.

The lawyer's plan is foiled. Turkey and Nippers continue to be their mechanical selves and in one of Melville's most wicked comic touches, the influence of Bartleby is shown to be contrary to the narrator's utilitarian desire. Turkey, Nippers, and the lawyer himself begin to echo Bartleby's key word (*prefer*) but without consciousness of what it is they say—they say the word without knowing they say the word; they deny saying the word even while saying the word, except for the lawyer, who reports that he had gotten "into the way of involuntarily using this word 'prefer' upon all sorts of not exactly suitable occasions" and that contact with the scrivener had "seriously affected me in a mental way. . . . What further and deeper aberration might it not yet produce?"

The lawyer is aware of his involuntary—which is to say, thoughtless—verbal action; aware that he is becoming like Turkey and Nippers, who speak Bartleby without awareness that they do so. Bartleby has had the effect of pulling the strings of their collective unconscious. Bartleby alone says "prefer" voluntarily, which is to say with full, free consciousness, with full and free will. The lawyer's plan is thwarted—Turkey and Nippers have acquired only the verbal veneer of freedom, and the lawyer, who prides himself on self-possession, fears losing himself to involuntary action or something even worse, but what would it be?

What allegorical role, precisely, does Melville intend Bartleby to play? As figure of the quintessentially free man, the nonconforming artist inside the nerve center of American capitalism, he would appear to represent disruption, perhaps a force of change. But change for what purpose? The free man here, as loose cannon, is the orphan who is free *from* but not free *to;* in his presence Turkey and Nippers can only replicate themselves in a new way; in unconscious imitation they become more thoroughgoing puppets, not new men for a new social order. The lawyer, on the other hand, who would seem to be Bartleby's proper allegorical antagonist, the Man of Business against the Serious Artist, himself drops into involuntary mode and fears that his imitative behavior presages some "further aberration," "deeper" yet than the undoing of his sanity. It's exactly at this point, in the contagion of "prefer," that Bartleby refuses any longer to copy. The lawyer asks him why and Bartleby, in what for him is an expansive moment, and while staring at the unbroken wall outside his work space, replies, "Do you not see the reason yourself?" The lawyer thinks Bartleby is referring to a temporary impairment of eyesight, owing to his "unexampled diligence" in copying over the past few weeks. But it is the dead wall itself, object of his reverie, that is the reason. At the moment in which the lawyer fears the worst, the onset of some ominous and general upheaval, Bartleby sinks into the deep passivity of his hopelessness before the White Wall of Commerce. Unlike Ahab, who is relentless to break through, Bartleby would appear to have given up. Whether it is *this* wall, or the wall of his actual prison at the Tombs, before which he stands and beneath which he will lie in death, Bartleby seems convinced (like the narrator) that the wall is of "amazing thickness," that it cannot be broken through, that it is everywhere and always the incarcerating fact of life.

Yet it is his act of giving up, paradoxically, that sends his disruptive influence even deeper into the society of Wall Street. And this moment in the text is both Melville's hopeful fantasy for social transformation *and* his despair for artistic praxis. Bartleby gives up scrivening just as his creator had. Melville's refusal to copy is the inaugurating moment of his original fiction, but he failed to make a dent. The culture simply ignored him. His fantasy, embodied in Bartleby's refusal to scriven, is that such refusal would send the society down the slope of radical change (further and deeper aberration), a fantasy toyed with for much of the last third of the tale until he undoes it and reveals the truth of the serious artist: that his effort results in total self-destructive failure. Melville's turn to the writing of original fiction is the biographical equivalent of Bartleby's allegorical turn into staring silence before the wall. Melville asks, in effect, if "serious" artistic desire is not in itself a disease equal in its virulent impact on the artist to the disease, the commercial context, which gave the primal wound to the artist and triggered his oppositional impulse. The disease that is commercial society begets not the artist as good doctor who would cure it but the suicidal artist. Bartleby, the original of Kafka's "Hunger Artist," refuses connection to a bad order, there is no other, and starves himself to death.

+ + +

The difficulty of Melville's novella is relieved less by reflection on the enigma of its title character—whose function is to represent, however darkly, an idea—than it is by reflection on Melville's narrator, a figure clearly not of his creator's self-projection, a character, rather, in a mode that Melville almost never worked—the realistic mode of the first person narrator, of psychological density, who tells inadvertently the story of himself.

Tellingly, the narrator complains that Bartleby is not "cheerfully industrious." Bartleby's unhappiness, which should be irrelevant in light of his huge productivity, is for some reason (*what* reason?) not irrelevant for this prudent man of business. He senses, we say in retrospect, though he does not know that he does, some danger in Bartleby's sadness. When Bartleby refuses to read proof, the narrator is brought to mind of that "mettlesome poet" of revolution, Byron, who could not be imagined doing such work. Bartleby must be mad, is the conclusion, yet he, the lawyer, feels "strangely disarmed, touched and disconcerted." "Strangely" because these feelings make no sense in the situation—they disarm the employer, they are not useful for business. The lawyer reports that he feels "browbeaten in some unprecedented and violently unreasonable" manner. On his side, he tells Bartleby, there is "common usage" and there is "common sense," and yet his faith in what he calls reason feels undermined; somehow, he senses, "all justice and reason are on the other side," though he cannot say what kind of reason, or counter reason, Bartleby represents. He's losing touch with what he knows as reason, feels ashamed to be "ignominiously repulsed by this lean, penniless wight," so why is it that he "burned to be rebelled against"?

When he discovers Bartleby in the office on a Sunday morning, and when Bartleby, outrageously, refuses to let him in, declaring, surely madly, that he is "occupied," the narrator feels "unmanned and yet tranquilly permits his hired clerk to dictate to him, and order him away from his own premises." Precisely at this point, when the structure of power relations has gone topsy-turvy, the narrator feels a not unpleasing sadness, a fraternal melancholy, the bond of a common humanity. It is the point of maximum danger, this bond with the Arch Refuser, but a point not long lingered over. Bartleby again refuses to read proof, and it is then that the narrator feels that he must be losing his mind and that some "deeper aberration" may be at hand. When Bartleby refuses to copy the narrator feels, or half feels, that the delicate bond of humanity is broken. In his heart, he would cast Bartleby out to a place alone, "absolutely alone in the universe." Bartleby is not yet, however, perfectly exorcised from the narrator's sympathies. As the Man of Business, whose identity is his manhood, and whose manhood is inseparable from his property rights, he puts to Bartleby the following questions, when Bartleby refuses to leave the premises:

> "Do you pay any rent?"
> "Do you pay my taxes?"
> "Is this property yours?"

Public opinion obtrudes; he fears scandal, worries, in the mode of his prudency, that Bartleby may claim possession of the office by "right of perpetual occupancy," has fears of clients leaving, fears of a mob riled into action—to do what?—by the strange scrivener's inaction. Yet, when Bartleby refuses to vacate, it is the narrator who meekly quits the premises and admits the "wondrous ascendancy" of Bartleby. "Wondrous" is correct: beyond understanding on the terrain of capital. Finally, unable to persuade Bartleby to leave, he decides to move his office and, upon leaving, reflects on the wonder of his enigmatic feelings: "I tore myself from him whom I had so longed to be rid of." The Man of Business cares for Bartleby, unfortunately. Bartleby, who does not move, is arrested as a vagrant.

His narrative tone unstable to the end, the narrator, who cannot act, and Bartleby, who does not act, are both acted on ("stabilized") by the social system, and the narrator is at last revealed not as Bartleby's antagonist but as his half-hearted ally, whose half-heartedness makes him the half-unwilling agent of the system: an exquisite image of psychological and moral paralysis, socially induced. In the final sentences, he gives us the rumor about Bartleby's former employment in the Dead Letter Office: the rumor, in allegorical light, of the Melvillean writer who sends his best to an audience that will never read it.

Though he never describes himself physically, we may imagine the narrator in the literary image of success of a bygone era: portly, slope-bellied, therefore rich. As for Bartleby's body, who eats almost nothing: his physical state of emaciation is the adequate image of his equally emaciated one-dimensional psychological reality. In Bartleby, Melville gives us a weightless character at the border of being and nonbeing. In this characterization, he does not fail as a writer who cannot make his central character vivid. Melville rather appears to have wanted to render an almost blank wisp of humanity, the point being that, as a figure of the serious artist who refuses to copy, who instead reaches for originality, Bartleby is emaciated in every way, a human blank, even on the threshold. Bartleby's actual and Melville's writerly death were inherent as the deep drifts of their lives, even as they scrivened: as if Melville's original writing were the equivalent of Bartleby's fatal stage of emaciation. Bartleby and Melville lurch deathward from the outset: unfed, unhoused, unparented, culturally homeless in a culture that they cannot escape, that will easily shrug off disruptive writers, bury them, and forget their names. These criminals of art, they scare no one.

The opposition held so easily, sometimes so sentimentally, by serious artists and their defenders after Melville, Art against Commerce, is subverted. *Bartleby* is a story of fraternal losers: the Unhappy Man of Art and the Unhappy Man of Business. And the winner? A Frankensteinian system subject to no intervention. It prefers not to.

+ + +

Melville's myth of himself as an orphan was triggered by actual family circumstances—his father dead when he was twelve, his mother (apparently) icily unavailable; J. M. Synge's comparable myth was based on an ideological decision to forsake his affluent Anglo-Irish heritage—his class, his Protestant religion—and subsequently to embrace what he called a "temperate nationalism." ("Everything Irish," Synge said without temperance, "became sacred.") And just as Melville's autobiographical myth fed his most significant writing, so did Synge's deliberately orphaned cultural life feed his major play, *The Playboy of the Western World*, whose most resonant episode occurs offstage, and before the play's beginning, when a motherless young man in the west of Ireland, legendary home of authentic Irish identity, in a rebellious rage kills, thinks he kills, his father-oppressor. On the evidence of the play's construction, Synge is arguably a vigorous Aristotelian: the mere telling of the plot is sufficient to give us the thrill of the play's action. But Synge's daring mixture of genres in *Playboy*—political allegory and disturbing comedy, featuring, in the final moment, a heroine grievously dispossessed of her love and the possibility of a free Ireland—would have presented to Aristotle's pristine literary categories a puzzlement impenetrable, however original.

+ + +

As the play opens, Pegeen Flaherty, "a wild-looking but fine girl," is discovered in a rough country pub, alone, writing an order for the materials to make her wedding dress. Shawn, the groom-to-be, enters. Without bothering to look up at him from her work (a telling indifference) she informs him that her father, Michael the publican, will go off with his friends to a wake and be gone until the next day, and she's afraid to be left by herself for the night. The ungallant Shawn, fearful of appearances, and most especially of what Father Reilly would say, refuses to stay with her. She scorns his timidity; this groom-to-be, clearly, is the Groom Undesirable. Enter "a slight young man," "tired and frightened and dirty," who speaks in a "small voice." Can this possibly be her knight in shining armor? It is Christy Mahon, who tells all present (Pegeen, Shawn, Michael, Michael's friends) that he's been on the road for days, a fugitive after having murdered his father. Improbably, this most unimpressive young man's statement instantly transforms his audience; they are in awe; their awe, in turn, instantly transforms him. Pegeen of the biting tongue quickly and derisively dismisses Shawn. On the strength of his murderous claim, the slight young man is elevated to the status of hero and, we guess, Groom Desirable. Before our eyes he grows large, gallant, and brave.

At the top of the second act, Christy—having been given shelter at the pub and a job as Michael's assistant—is discovered alone, "bright and cheerful." He says, "I'll be growing fine from this day." Enter three young country girls—the word has gone forth—bearing gifts for the parricide. What's more, they will enter the hero in the sporting contests to take place later that day. He is, after all, a likely "playboy," who would vanquish all. And why not? Is he not a parricide? The parricide, moreover, is father to the poet: Christy tells his story to the admiring girls and reveals himself to be an artist of narrative and lyric command, who fabricates out of his extravagant arias just the sort of hero who could slay the father-oppressor and thereby bring an entire village to his feet. Pegeen and Christy, mutually transformed, fall quickly in love. Shawn, now the blocking agent to true love, brings Christy a one-way ticket to America and fine clothes. Christy runs him out, but not before taking the clothes. He swaggers to the door, tightening his belt. He opens the door, spots a dead man outside the pub, then staggers back. A second blocking agent, Christy's murdered father, appears. Christy darts in, hiding behind the door.

The third and final act opens with reports of Christy's exploits on the fields of sport. The victor in every contest, this champion Playboy of the Western World is raised up high on the shoulders of his admirers and enters to accept his prizes. Then, the dark news is told: dispensation has been granted; Shawn and Pegeen may now, with her father's approval, marry. Pegeen refuses; her fierce champion frightens Shawn, blocking agent number 1, into fleeing; Michael accepts Christy because, as he says, "a daring fellow is a jewel of the world." Blocking agent number 2, Old Mahon, presumably hoodwinked by a widow with designs on Christy into leaving for good, returns; Pegeen, disillusioned, now that her groom-champion has been revealed not to have done the daring deed of parricide, recoils and rejects him. Christy, intent on doing the job properly, once and for all, chases his father out of the pub (and off stage); Christy reenters and is tied up in order to be dragged off to the police for the crime of murder. Pegeen scorches his leg with a burning sod. Old Mahon again returns, yet again unkilled, this time to go off happily with his son, now his son's slave. The way is cleared for the proper conclusion of a dramatic comedy—with a mean twist. The unfortunate marriage of Shawn and Pegeen looms and the play ends with Pegeen's deep Irish lament: "Oh my grief, I've lost him surely. I've lost the only Playboy of the Western World."

+ + +

The plot of *Playboy* is funny, sad, and at key points absurd. While the conjoining of such qualities has precedent in the comic tradition, it is Synge's provoking originality as a playwright to have placed his most absurd incident—the celebration of the parricide—in a context of sharply observed peasant realism. These are authentic characters, and this is authentic "speech" (not phony writing), Synge says in the preface to his play. It is an authenticity that emerges from the actual local earth of the west of Ireland: not to be found in the "elaborate books" of modern writers of metropolitan—he means, as Wordsworth did before him, "artificial"—consciousness.

The riots occasioned by *Playboy*'s premiere performances in Dublin were reactions to Synge's unromanticized and often satiric renderings of peasant life. His characters are crude, self-centered, and consistently unheroic. They are not, as turn of the century nationalist propaganda would have it, saints of pure Irishness struggling to free themselves from the yoke of empire. Insofar as the rioters were reacting to Synge's salty portraits, particularly of the women—the historical evidence suggests that they were—then they were merely pious. Insofar as the rioters may have intuited that Synge's judgment of the chances of successful revolt, driven by the peasant class, was pessimistic in the extreme, then those rioters had understood Synge very well.

Pegeen's fear of loneliness is given immediate political resonance. She longs for the dead—the old insurrectionaries who were also poet-storytellers of "Holy Ireland," while she fears and loathes Ireland's twin masters, "the thousand [British] militia" who walk "idle in the land" and the Catholic Church, which she scorns through Shawn, whose repeated invocations of Father Reilly she mockingly imitates. Her father, who should protect her but instead goes off to an all-night drinking party—an Irish wake—prefers Shawn not for his Catholic pieties but for his financial solidity: Ireland's third master, what Yeats contemptuously called the "greasy till."

In this context, Pegeen assumes the traditional (female) symbolic role of "Holy Ireland" herself, awaiting liberation by a heroic male when Christy makes his initial entrance. Before he reveals his crime, Michael and his friends make various guesses, each one of which speak of an urge to strike back at the imperial oppressor within. Synge has now plunged us beneath "plot" to "action," that dynamic life of spirit that is here, in this play, the mythic movement of indigenous Irish desire toward freedom.

The celebration and elevation of the parricide, absurd in this play's realistic register, is credible at its allegorical level. Beneath the gritty texture of peasant life moves the spirit of revolt, a yen for political violence led by a romantic literary figure, awaiting the slightest excuse to erupt. And Christy, it is clear from Synge's stage directions, is indeed the slightest of excuses. In his actuality, he is the least likely candidate for the role of poet-rebel; as Pegeen says it, those "fine fiery fellows with great rages when their temper's aroused." It is in the allegorical register, and only there, that the scheming Widow Quin makes sense: "There's great temptation in a man did slay his da." The private and the public, the romantic and the political, are fused in the figure of the parricide, and it is very much to the point that in his actuality Christy is too light for the part. The point being here, as everywhere in Synge's play, double: comic as well as political. Nevertheless, desire for liberation would have him for the part. Therefore, he will play the part because in the eye of desire he's perfectly cast. Inspired by his claim to have murdered his father, symbol of all political oppression, the community-as-artist would sculpt the meager materials of desire (Christy himself) into the heroic realization of its hope.

Synge's gift for playing off desire's transformation of the real against the stubborn shabbiness of the real is the basis of the deep action of *Playboy;* it is the source of Synge's humor (Christy seeks fame and creaturely comforts); it is Synge's way of delineating the ever-present political unconscious of Irish life; it is the ground of his acerbic evaluation of nationalist hopes for Ireland. Desire will remain locked inside the fantasy life of the Irish because its object—here represented by Christy—is hopelessly inadequate to its need for heroism. All of which is to say that political desire, as long as it is focused on heroic saviors, will not emerge as act and achievable intention, not in Synge's vision of Ireland. This would be the better reason, were it understood, for opening night rioting by enraged nationalists.

+ + +

The action that sweeps characters and community toward a unified destiny is conservative, not revolutionary. Christy the parricide, who teases into thought the ravishing (and deluded) idea of the Slayer of All Unjust Authority, private and public, cannot, in fact, kill the father. The Father is unkillable. The criminal whose violent act launches him into the role of poetic storyteller is no criminal, and his transgressive storytelling is only storytelling, lyric fiction divorced from reality. At the play's end, the traditional power relation of father and son is not destroyed; it is reversed, so that the son may now play the role of oppressor. Pegeen (or Ireland) whose lover and freedom are fused in the single hopeful figure of the poet–father killer, is divested in one stroke of romantic love and the promise of freedom. For Synge, they are the same: both without reference to reality. She will marry Shawn (or Catholicism), who in tandem with British imperialism will jointly rule the Irish. Shawn alone gets what he wants. And Pegeen's final, terrible cry—she's lost "the only Playboy of the Western World"—is shockingly bitter. Christy—"a small low fellow," in his father's words—pathetic Christy, is the world's only playboy. Where does this leave Ireland? At the end, we find the community where it was at the beginning, before the onset of hope, which is shown, in this play, to be indistinguishable from unrelieved, and unrelievable, pain.

+ + +

I am quite simply not a good person.

WITTGENSTEIN'S NEPHEW

In the canon of loose artistic cannons, the Austrian Thomas Bernhard may be the loosest of them all: a nonstop literary smasher whose unparagraphed novels unleash tornadoes of abuse—violent criticism of everything that constitutes modern Austria, with no accompanying alternative vision of revolution or reform, no hopeful imagination of reconstructive possibility for the "miserable shitspot" of his native country. Like Melville's *Bartleby,* the writing of Bernhard is a plunge into nihilism; unlike Melville, whose tale goes with resignation into darkest night, Bernhard rages with formidable vituperative—and comedic—energy against the dying of the light: fifteen novels, eighteen stage plays, six book-length autobiographical pieces, a few volumes of melancholy lyric poetry, several screen plays.

In public statements he regularly attacked major figures and institutions of Austrian culture and politics—including the revered Elias Canetti, a Nobel Prize winner, and former chancellors Bruno Kreisky and Kurt Waldheim, the latter of jackbooted past. For a time, the sales of his novel *The Woodcutters* were halted by a well-known composer (and ex-friend) who believed himself (for good reason) slandered by the book, a scandal-engendering act that generated heated press in Austria and Germany for several weeks. His most spectacular violation, *Heldenplatz,* a black rewriting of *The Cherry Orchard* in which not a trace of Chekhov's guarded sympathy survives, was produced by Vienna's Burgtheater for the repertory season 1988–89—Bernhard died in February of 1989—and it required, on opening night, thanks to press leaks of some incendiary passages of the script, two hundred policemen stationed around all entrances of the theater prior to curtain time. The play—set in 1988—was written, stated Bernhard, in his customary manner, to commemorate the fiftieth anniversary of Austria's annexation to Hitler's Reich. "There are more Nazis in Vienna now," says one of the characters, "than in thirty-eight." Heldenplatz (Heroes Square): the monumental space in front of the Hapsburg Palace where Hitler and his troops were greeted by the greatest number of Austrians ever to gather in one place when they arrived in Vienna on March 15, 1938. "Only ninety percent of my colleagues," says one of the characters, "are Nazis."

"On opening night," writes his English translator, Gitta Honegger, "Right Wing activists [earliest reviewers] dumped horse manure in front of the theater." Another reviewer, of the more conventional sort, with no Nazi sympathy, wrote that Bernhard "makes a Viennese Jew bark like a German shepherd." This reviewer forgot that Bernhard was always an equal opportunity abuser: his badly damaged Jews were champion abusers themselves. Are they not Austrians? The opening night performance concluded with a forty-minute standing ovation—a fact not easy to mesh with the writer's prevailing nihilism. Forty minutes from the Viennese. Says one of the characters, "Every Viennese is a born mass-murderer."

+ + +

Key episodes in the Bernhard biography constitute a virtual recipe for the making of a loose cannon: His mother gave birth to him in 1931 in Holland, in a home for unwed mothers, where she was driven from Catholic Austria. His father not only deserted them but never acknowledged Thomas as his son, and Bernhard never knew him. He remembers his mother mainly as the deliverer of terrible sentences: "You've ruined my life!" "You're nothing!" "I'm ashamed of you!" "You're a bum like your father!" "You're worthless!" He was raised largely by his maternal grandparents in crowded circumstances in and around Salzburg, where his schooling took place in a Nazi-run institution that, after the war, was continued under Catholic administration. Bernhard's fiction would link the two regimes as indistinguishably fascist: the deep twin expressions, he would insist repeatedly, of the Austrian character.

In his late teens he developed an interest in classical singing, was headed for a career as an operatic bass-baritone, when he became seriously ill with pleurisy, was incorrectly (criminally, he would say) diagnosed as terminally tubercular, and consigned for five years to a wretched hospital for the terminally ill with tuberculosis, where he fulfilled his doctor's hopes and progressed to tuberculosis. His plans for a career in opera destroyed, his career as a chronic patient took off, fueled by the cardiovascular diseases that debilitated him for the rest of his life. He turned inward, to a life of writing, whose single repulsive object was the world that had denied him nourishing connection to something larger than himself—inward to a self for which, in its various impoverishments, he had difficulty feeling anything but self-loathing; an abandoned child who longs for approval from the world that has orphaned him. Those who give literary awards, he writes in *Wittgenstein's Nephew,* wish to piss on the recipients. If you accept the award, you deserve to be pissed on. He was awarded many literary prizes, and he accepted them all.

+ + +

Fecal references abound in Bernhard because the premise of all of his writing is that the world is a "mindless, cultureless," and unalterable "cesspool." Modern Austria, consequently, is his metaphor for modern

Western cultures. The cesspool world produces in a few thinking persons—there are *very* few of these in Bernhard's work—dangerous lifelong reactions of rebellion; dangerous because lives driven by extreme pitches of rebellion can only subvert the body and mind of the rebel, producing eventually chronic and finally fatal physical and mental diseases—a distinction that Bernhard collapses. In *Wittgenstein's Nephew,* the most elegant representation of his aesthetic in its psychosocial context, Bernhard the apparent nihilist son of Dostoevsky's Underground Man raises this unavoidable question: Why go on? Why not give into his lung disease as his special friend Paul Wittgenstein had given into his mental disease? And if that doesn't do the trick, why not die by one's own hand?

At the outset of *Wittgenstein's Nephew* we find Paul and Thomas in hospital, separated by two hundred yards, with Paul in the Ludwig pavilion for the mad and Thomas in the Hermann pavilion for chest patients, the two sites rendered constantly in sentences of parallel construction. Unlike Paul, who is dominated by illness, the indomitable Thomas shrewdly cherishes his rebellion-produced illness and thereby *flourishes* by exploiting it: this flourishing, which takes its origin in disease; this disease which takes its origin in rebellion; this rebellion which takes it origin in the cesspool. In disease, Thomas finds his true identity.

What exactly is this flourishing from corruption? Bernhard calls it his art. So when he tells us in *Wittgenstein's Nephew* that illness is the "mainspring" of his existence, he tells us, in effect, that the mainspring of his existence is the cesspool, that he could not come to himself as an artist without it, that the cesspool is his muse. Among the artistic loose cannons who require *mondo merda* in order to be artists, Bernhard may be the most luminous.

What is the nature and function of Bernhard's art? In *Heldenplatz* he gives us two metafictional clues:

1. The thinking person cannot help but vomit first thing
   in the morning.
2. reality is so bad
   it defies description

no writer has ever described reality
as it really is
that's the horror

The romantic theory of art as expressive act—the pressing out of interior process—is here redefined. To write is to vomit. What has come into us under cover of nourishment is in fact poison. Since Paul published no art or philosophy, he could only live his madness—for music, philanthropy, coffeehouses, and Formula One racing—could merely live it and was therefore killed in mind and body by it. But Thomas the artistic exploiter of his nausea could puke it out, press out a puke rhetoric that bears witness (just as actual vomit does) to the corruption that has entered us as food for life; bears witness to the crimes of society. Writing is immediate therapy, a relief of rage nausea but also a returning of the favor: Bernhard's immensely productive writing life would contaminate in lucid vomit language that which caused him to vomit, with no hope that such reactive art can change a thing. Society, not the artist, is the criminal and cannot be rehabilitated. The real is so bad that it cannot even be described—that is the horror relentlessly registered in Bernhard's work. Paradoxically, precisely this constantly vomited horror, pressed out every morning by the thinking person, becomes a powerful, if indirect, representation and indictment of what cannot be represented in the traditional manner. The style and form of his fiction is the organic expression of his aesthetic of expression. His unbroken—unparagraphed—prose is the image of a voice in ceaseless monologue, a perfectly sustained legato flowing from the throat, eloquent channel of Bernhard's nausea, who in this way had his career as an opera singer after all.

+ + +

The Wittgenstein family, prime movers of the Austrian steel cartel, billionaire arms manufacturers whose sole values, writes Bernhard, are wealth and property, has nothing but contempt for the life of the mind and regarded Ludwig Wittgenstein, the most influential philosopher of the twentieth century, as a "*shameless character,*" the "*fool of the family.*"

Bernhard's title implies a story in itself: Paul the madman, with his unpublished genius and endless passion for music, has one relative only—Ludwig; neither had any others. Both were spiritually abandoned by the family, just as Bernhard was abandoned spiritually (and literally) by his. *Wittgenstein's Nephew,* with its open use of real people—Thomas, Paul, and Ludwig—is in effect the creation of a new Austrian family of artist-philosopher orphans. Thomas, Paul, and Ludwig: pitted against Austria and the materialistic Wittgensteins who hid their materialism behind patronage of the arts. Thomas, Paul, and Ludwig: relatives, then, not by blood but by affiliations of rebellion, disease, and highest achievements of mind.

Like all of his novels and plays, *Wittgenstein's Nephew* is a story of extremity—Bernhard has no other story to tell—of two men who find themselves in utmost physical and mental danger, because of Austria; because of the maximum intensity of their impossible needs, marked to the core by the world's denial of what is needed and cannot be granted by and in this world; because neither Paul nor Thomas can supply what is needed from the self—there is nothing inside but defeated idealism masked as rage; there is simply nothing in the self and, unlike God, they cannot create ex nihilo; because one of them will fail friendship; because isolation and fear of death cancel everything. What is most required—the nurturing love of home, familial and cultural—is not possible. Homelessness is the negative foundation of Bernhard's extremity: "The truth is that I am happy *only when I am sitting in the car,* between the place I have just left and the place I am driving to. I am happy only when I am traveling; when I arrive I am suddenly the unhappiest person imaginable. Basically I am one of those people who cannot bear to be anywhere and are happy only between places."

In the primordial cesspool, primordial extremity of reaction, which gives birth to a rhetoric of extremity, is in evidence on virtually every page of *Wittgenstein's Nephew:* "I am happy only when . . ."; "the unhappiest person imaginable . . ."; "at that time I found it quite simply impossible, without Paul, to have any conversation about music or philosophy or politics or mathematics . . ."; "I can only describe these places [in Austria] as miserable shitspots, which thoroughly deserve this description, if

not an even shittier one . . . no one with intellectual pretensions could possibly exist in a place where the *Neue Zürcher Zeitung* is unobtainable. . . . We should live only in a place where we can at least get the *Neue Zürcher Zeitung*, I said, and Paul wholeheartedly agreed . . ."; "I have never learned anything new [at the literary coffeehouses] but only been annoyed and irritated and pointlessly depressed. At the Sacher I was never irritated or depressed, or even annoyed . . ."; "From my early youth I have regarded the ability to read English and French books and newspapers as the greatest advantage I possess. What would my world be like . . . if I had to rely on the German papers which are for the most part little more than garbage sheets—to say nothing of Austrian newspapers, which are not newspapers at all but mass circulation issues of unusable toilet paper. . . ." In this context, a sudden turn of the rhetoric of extremity to ruthless self-evaluation: "I find myself unsupportable, and even more unsupportable is a whole horde of writers and brooders like myself. I avoid literature whenever possible, because whenever possible I avoid myself. . . ."

Most of all, though, the extremity of his friendship with Paul, "the most valuable relationship I have ever had with another man." Both in hospital, Bernhard suddenly fears the loss of Paul—either through his (Paul's) death or through his own: "I suddenly longed for this man, the only man I had ever been able to talk to in a way that was congenial to me . . . what I have to have if I am to go on existing." Like his illness, which gave birth to his art, and was therefore the "mainspring" of his existence, Paul also is the mainspring of his existence. Somehow—how?—two mainsprings. But the conversations with Paul were not the sine qua non. More than the talk, what Bernhard says "he shall never forget" were those "wordless musical evenings I spent with him." A deeper concord, then, through the mediation of music—the nonreferential art, the transcendence of all that is phenomenal, according to Bernhard's philosophical heroes, Schopenhauer and Kierkegaard: union with Paul in inhuman silence of the noumenal.

The mainspring is the cesspool; the mainspring is illness; the mainspring is art; the mainspring is friendship: with so many candidates for the mainspring, the truth of Bernhard's despair emerges. There is no mainspring, and this godless man reaches in poignant contradiction through the aesthetics of music for what is beyond the cesspool, reaches for that which he does not believe in.

+ + +

He who most of all needs love cannot love and fears its touch: "I was actually afraid that he might *suddenly* rush in and embrace me and cry his heart out. I loved him, but I did not want to be embraced by him, and I hated it when he cried his heart out to me at the age of fifty-nine or sixty." A description of Bernhard's fears, in 1967, when the two friends found themselves struck down in their respective pavilions. In exquisite—and strangely funny—self-laceration for which he has no remedy, Bernhard comments: "It had long been clear that anyone who behaved like this was dangerously sick." In Paul's final days, Bernhard tells us that out of a "base instinct for self-preservation" he had shunned his friend. He wanted to dissociate himself from the inevitable and only truth he knew, the truth of death, which is what he was afraid of being brought face to face with. He abandoned Paul. Was in another country when Paul died. Has not, until this day, he writes in the final sentence, visited Paul's grave.

In *Old Masters,* Bernhard's eighty-two-year-old alter ego, a music critic of the first rank, tells us that books, the greatest of them, music, philosophy—all of which had meant everything to him—became of no use, offered no consolation, were completely ridiculous in the crucial moment when he lost his wife and found himself, with all his Shakespeare and Kant and Mozart and Tintoretto, alone "in an utterly horrible sense." Only after his wife's death, when his knowledge of her worth is worthless, does he realize that the life of the mind is nothing, that life with his wife was everything, that she was the only consolation. The secret of Bernhard's nihilistic writing is that there *is* something, only one thing, that matters, that it is not nothing, but he cannot have it, because when he does have it, he cannot honor it. It was when he was on the verge of suicide, he writes, that Paul Wittgenstein came into his life, at the height of his despair, to make life endurable. Then, in the harshest moment of his self-critique, he tells us that bitter experience inhibited him from including the living among those who mean everything. Paul Wittgenstein, who had made his life worth living, could not be properly loved: a reflection in guilt, written after Paul's death.

What Bernhard writes while detailing his abandonment of Paul—"I am quite simply not a good person"—is the definition of his irremediable extremity: my badness is my ontological condition; it is timeless, not, therefore, subject to the actions that I might perform in time. No deeds of mine, including deeds of love, can alter who I am, so why should I perform them? And I have not. In all but words, Bernhard says, There is another cesspool: *c'est moi.*

Melville's Bartleby, the artist who in effect commits suicide; Synge's Pegeen, who abandons all hope for love and a liberated Ireland; Bernhard's Bernhard, self-conscious wallower in self-loathing: three faces of transgressive despair.

7. THE LAST MANIACAL FOLLY OF HEINRICH VON KLEIST (A FICTION)

On the afternoon of November 21, 1811, the writer Heinrich von Kleist was the perpetrator of a murder and the victim of a suicide. This double deed was his greatest crime and most infamous work of art, the enactment at last on the stage of the real world of what he had suggested in his play *Penthesilea.* He and Henriette Vogel were found lying in their blood, shot to death, approximately one hundred paces from the main road, on the hill close by the so-called little Wannsee. According to the official report, "Both were in a small trench of approximately one foot in depth and three in diameter." The lady was lying on her back, and Kleist was kneeling between her feet, his left hand lying limply over his left knee. Beside her hip, his head rested on his right hand, which still held the pistol barrel pointed toward his mouth. This writer-director had scouted the location for what would turn out to be one of the earliest acts of performance art, violent death as art, in the autumn of 1810, when he met the poet Fouqué on the banks of the Wannsee, where they clasped hands in token of friendship and joyous association. And once before, in 1801, he met some friends there, and they imagined the best way to go: earlier preproduction. His approach involved rocks in the pockets, floating in a skiff, gazing up at the sky, a single shot to the head, and just rolling over. Just rolling over. He auditioned a poet with whom he was casually acquainted, Karoline von Günderrode, for the role of Henriette Vogel, the woman he would eventually murder in his final production. But Karoline will prefer to perform her own suicide as a solo, killing herself for love with a knife in her bare breast and a towel weighted down with stones around her neck, a crime quite different from murder.

+ + +

A Dialogue on the Subject of Maniacal Follies

Teacher: **H. v Kleist,** failed playwright, failed lover
Student: **K. v Günderrode,** poet, failed lover

Winter 1804. A chance meeting on the riverbank.

H. v Kleist: By way of background: This concerns the aftermath of my so-called Mainz episode, where I at last collapsed, ill, and for nearly five months kept alternately to my bed or my room. (In between trips to Paris to witness the setting up of the French empire, complete with plot scares, and after my maniacal folly, or follies, as I tried twice to join the would-be, soon-to-be emperor Bonaparte in his assault on England.) Mainz, the last outpost before facing the music at home, the cacophony of my family and my late, great, failed expectations. I guess it's fair to say I become ill when I cannot deal with matters at hand. Either I become ill and can't get out of bed, or I travel in several directions in rapid succession, or both.

On this my strange journey I met a fellow traveler, a lady. Since then I have lost all insight into the causes of my illness. I think of illness as a journey, a slow boat along the river of the mind, or a strenuous climb up the mountain of the body. How I wish it were someone else's body. Perhaps this dialogue will illuminate how certain things followed on certain others. After it was all over, I finally did what everybody else wanted me to do in the first place, but that didn't last very long either. And then I did what I wanted to do.

The Dialogue

My first glimpse of her: she stands on the brink of the river Rhine, upon a dead fir tree, uprooted, holding in her hand a comb. Her hair is loose as if for washing. Hearing me approach, she turns, looking full of fear—or is it loathing?

Heinrich: I've disturbed you—

Karoline: (shaking her head) How wonderful to stand completely alone under an overcast sky gazing out over what I wish were an endless expanse of water, but is only a river with an all too visible opposite bank.

Heinrich: Should I go?

Karoline: No, we can be alone together.

Heinrich: I'm afraid it's a condition with which I'm all too familiar.

Karoline: (turns back to the river) I wish the water were endless; that opposite bank is interrupting my thoughts.

Heinrich: It wants something?

Karoline: Recognition, perhaps. Or it's offering something in return.

Heinrich: Redemption?

Karoline: What is it about here that makes us want to get to there?

Heinrich: The dead tree you're standing on makes me think about losing my balance.

Karoline: About falling?

Heinrich: Yes, if you don't mind—(he offers her his hand and helps her to steadier ground) I saw you here yesterday. You were waving at something.

Karoline: Impossible.

Heinrich: Did you see a ship?

Karoline: I come here every day just to gaze.

Heinrich: At?

Karoline: If you ask then I was wrong.

Heinrich: About what?

Karoline: I thought you could see it, too.

Heinrich: See what?

Karoline: The future.

Heinrich: I feel as if my eyelids have been cut off. I see no sign of life, but I hear it in the water, in the wind, in the movement of the clouds, in the cries of the birds.

Karoline: So you do sense the river inside the river. If only I could be satisfied here in this place, drink in the coolness and sustenance of the river, not fixate on what lies beyond.

Heinrich: It's so quiet here. The river looks like a blushing virgin.

Karoline: There was a storm here this morning.

Heinrich: I should tell you I've been here before. I used to take a skiff and row to the middle of the river, lie on the floor, and gaze at the sky forgetting the entire world. The water had its way with me, plunging into me a flood of daydreams.

Karoline: I can't look at a body of water without it reminding me of death. But then, I could say that about so many things.

Heinrich: Would you like to travel with me to the other side?

Karoline: What would be the difference between there and here?

Heinrich: (taking out a pair of glasses) Here, put these on.

Karoline: They're green.

Heinrich: That's the point. (She puts them on.) Now you can't tell if what you're seeing is really green or it only looks green.

Karoline: I keep falling in love with men who lose interest in me.

Heinrich: Totally?

Karoline: No, erotically. They stay interested in my mind.

Heinrich: I understand the problem.

Karoline: Then they marry somebody else.

Heinrich: I was engaged once, but it was my mental interest that flagged. I kept thinking that if I could stimulate mental interest, the erotic would follow suit. Frankly, I think she was relieved when I broke it off.

Karoline: I write to dream away the present and live in my imagination.

Heinrich: I write because I can't not write. I can't write, and I can't not write. I get terrible headaches that make me lose my sense of direction.

Karoline: My headaches make me blind.

Heinrich: Let us return to the river. Once upon a time I committed a folly. Actually, more than once, but I wish to speak here of one particular folly. After I tore off my own pair of green glasses, I hit upon a brilliant method of self-destruction. My brother Leopold, two friends, Rühle and Gleissenberg from my old Potsdam regiment, and I took an excursion together. To a lake. Self-annihilation was not the first thing on my mind that day, nor was it the last. Looking at that body of water, that lake, that little Wannsee, it occurred to me that my soul was a skiff, abandoned on an infinite sea of desire, in a sterile field of cares and ignorance, among the mirages of knowledge—I had just discovered the philosopher Kant, you see. So I was at the mercy of the sea's great madness, as it were. The spiritual sail I contemplated raising so that the breath of God might bring me to port, was not faith, but the goal of self-destruction.

Karoline: Was that the first time you had thought of it?

Heinrich: That was the first time I had sketched the scene. This obsession with killing myself is what constitutes my idée fixe, the essence of my melancholia. Dr. Wedekind here in Mainz is observing me to see if I am mad because I am interested in the life of unreason flashing like lightning in the sky of reasonable life. I don't wish to be liberated from my insanity, if I am insane. I want to realize it in my writing. Communicate with what is deepest in myself and with what is most solitary.

Karoline: Isn't it ironic, though, that we seem to be able to communicate with what is most solitary while talking to someone else?

Heinrich: That's why I've always wanted to do it with somebody else, not alone.

Karoline: Do you think I should do it?

Heinrich: Let's rehearse.

(They board a skiff moored below.)

The most important thing is that the result must be painstakingly ensured in advance. We row to the middle of the lake, load one of our pockets with stones.

Karoline: They would have to be heavy, the stones. Rocks, really.

Heinrich: Seat yourself so you fall backward upon firing. (They sit.)

Karoline: In case of a misfire.

Heinrich: Exactly, that way you would, at least, drown.

Karoline: And what would be the cause?

Heinrich: The cause, the cause . . . I could do it to celebrate, I could do it out of despair, it wouldn't matter. On that occasion, on the little Wannsee, I was shattered to realize that whatever Truth I might acquire here is not Truth after my death. Truth is nowhere on earth. It may never follow me into the grave. All is vanity. My lakeside folly was yet another attempt to distract myself, relieve myself. I walked there in the pouring rain and pressed my friends to my breast. The rain helped numb me.

Karoline: The mistake you make is in thinking of Truth as a possession at all. We take nothing with us to our graves.

Heinrich: I am unspeakably poor.

Karoline: If I am mad, my madness, on the other hand, is one of desperate passion.

Heinrich: Madness is no more than the derangement of the imagination.

I came here suffering from an idée fixe that I must bring about my own death because I had failed to write a great work. This was the occasion of a constantly renewed sadness. I tried to join Napoleon's forces, but he wouldn't take me. Melancholia is madness at the limits of its powerlessness; it never reaches violence. We are choked vessels full of heavy clogged blood.

Karoline: I'm used to that.

Heinrich: Movement of thought provoked to a standstill so that the state of my mind mirrors the state, excuse the expression, of my bowels—utter turgidity.

Karoline: It's different for women.

Heinrich: Do you have problems getting out of bed?

Karoline: Tremendous. Sadness and fear.

Heinrich: Fear I won't be able to bring about my own death. Sadness at the failure of my work.

Karoline: End result: Nausea.

Heinrich: Obstruction of mind, bowels, imagination.

Karoline: Let's row a little further. (They do.) My father died when I was six and at the age of seventeen I was confined in a convent. Somehow, surrounded by women, I managed to develop manly desires.

Heinrich: For example?

Karoline: First and foremost, the desire to write. Unfortunately, I had no money, but having money does not usually bring about the desire to write. A conundrum.

Heinrich: I have no money either. If it weren't for my sister, I'd be finished.

Karoline: I have no such sister. And the beautiful death of the battle-field—

Heinrich: What I looked for with Napoleon—

Karoline: That, too, is beyond my short reach.

Heinrich: Such deaths are usually suicides in my family and suicide requires no military post. I quit the military because officers can't be human beings.

Karoline: But there is at least the possibility of expressing one's independence in the military.

Heinrich: Not to my way of thinking. That's why I turned to writing. And that was after I tried education. You only want the military because you can't have it. I don't want it because my family expects it. When I wanted to enlist they wouldn't take me. And so it goes.

Karoline: If they had admitted me, I would have stayed.

Heinrich: And never written a line of poetry.

Karoline: I want love. I can't make money from writing. I'm trapped by poverty.

Heinrich: A man trapped in a woman's body. He wants to fight and kill.

Karoline: My mother was a secret writer who couldn't use her own name.

Heinrich: Lie on your back on the floor. (She does.) Look up.

Karoline: Death is the place of hope, union, escape from pain and solitude.

Heinrich: You wouldn't have to use a gun.

Karoline: A dagger would do.

Heinrich: (lying down beside her) I don't want to go alone. I asked my friend Pfuel to go with me. He refused, repeatedly.

Karoline: (turning to him) Why not go alone? Death isn't final. It's a chemical process, a separation of the powers, but not a destroyer.

Heinrich: You only think men enjoy the freedom to guide their own lives while women are bound by want and custom. Roman suicide was a form of moral and political behavior. English suicide is an illness because they kill themselves without reason. They kill themselves and they are happy. What about German suicide? The French think Germans kill themselves capriciously because metaphysical enthusiasm without object or useful end predominates.

Karoline: Isn't thinking too much about the life to come an object? Now as to whether or not it's useful . . .

Heinrich: Goethe's hero Werther killed himself for love. The French think the Germans need a political system calculated to open a career to men who are worthy of being patriots. So maybe Napoleon has in mind that he will provide us with such a system. (They are close enough to kiss.)

Karoline: The erotic identity unrealized, derailed. The writerly identity underrealized. Happiness unachieved. Delirium. Lira—furrow. De lira. Moved out of the furrow. Delirium. Do we have a disease of the head?

Heinrich: Is suicide succumbing to madness?

Karoline: Madness is the absence of a work of art.

Heinrich: But what about suicide itself as the ultimate work of art? The work of art is the sheer cliff over the abyss of the work's absence. The sheer cliff over the abyss of the artist's madness. So it all depends on where you're standing at the time. The work endlessly drives madness to its limits.

Karoline: It's getting dark.

Heinrich: I think it's hopeless and no good going on.

Karoline: (not opening her eyes) I agree.

Heinrich: (after a few moments) Look at me.

(*After a moment she does, but her eyes just slits because of the glare. He bends over her to get them in the shadow and they open.*)

(Pause. Low.) Let me in.

(*They drift in and stick among the rushes. He lies across her with his face in her breasts and his hand on her. They lie there without moving. But under them all moved, and moved them, gently, up and down, and from side to side.*)

Past midnight. Never knew such silence.

Karoline: The earth might be uninhabited.

Heinrich: Are you ready to go in?

Karoline: Come, Darkness, embrace me in night
That my lips may drink in new delight.
Cover yourself in Night, it stills your longing
And heals your pain, like Lethe's cool tides.
(*They continue floating gently downstream as the lights fade to black.*)

+ + +

Some years later I spent several months in the insane asylum at Bayreuth. This sojourn almost drove me mad. Because they wouldn't let me write. All exercises of the imagination were excluded as being in complicity with the passions, the desires, or all delirious delusions. The directors and staff of the asylum regularly invited me and several other patients to "tea-parties" where we could observe as well as be observed. Just as at such events in the life outside the institution, I was the perennial Stranger, reduced to performing. My most natural aspect was as a spy, a fly on the wall, a disappearing act. Once I was, in point of fact, wrongly arrested and imprisoned for being a spy, a political spy, which I was not. I was not insane either; I was merely the representative of an Age of Insanity.

An attempt to poison myself precipitated my stay in the asylum. One of my friends found me unconscious from an overdose of opium. My original intention was to use it to poison Napoleon. But somehow I had gotten sidetracked and used it on myself instead. This was my only solo attempt. I wonder if I felt more, or less, happy in the madhouse. Less, or more, myself. It was only for a couple of months. I know I believed that the disturbed could not be restored among others like themselves. But I wasn't in fact among others like myself.

The inmates took it upon themselves to perform my play *Penthesilea.* I had been reciting it aloud from memory as a form of meditation, and they liked what they heard. This constituted the premiere, as it were. The asylum—as good a place as any to try to draw the borderlines of sanity—housed an abundance of women ripe to play the Amazons, particularly apt to realize the violence and sensuality with a heightened vigor unknown to the society at large. The attendants took on some of the men's roles. At times events did go out of control and restraint had to be applied.

I have enclosed among my papers a letter from my dear friend, Dahlmann. Dahlmann, an esteemed historian, traveled with me on a double passport (like a married couple!), and was with me during a time when I had theoretically disappeared—mid July to the end of October 1809. It was during this time that I was interred, as it were, at the asylum at Bayreuth. It turns out I had to miss the performance for reasons I will not disclose, so Dahlmann, who did in fact attend as audience, graciously

provided me with details of the event. I believe that if Dahlmann thinks the play good even as performed by lunatics, it must be so.

+ + +

My dear Heinrich,
We are ushered into the bath hall of the asylum where we take our seats on a platform assembled to accommodate me (as your wife, or is it husband?—I'm never sure which), family members of other patients, and the director of the asylum. I am allowed to bear witness only because of our double passport and your incapacity on this particular day. The bathhouse seems the perfect venue for Water and Fire to come together in deadly combat.

In the opening moments the bell tolls. Patients are sitting, lying, and bathing. Suddenly a fight erupts among the male and female patients at the rear of the white tiled room. This conveniently gives the impression of Greeks and Amazons fighting each other without knowing why just as at the opening of your play. They go so far as to bite each other's throats (like vampires) before the nurses interrupt the melee, push the patients back, and sing them a soothing song.

The director agrees at the last moment to stand in as Odysseus for one of the patients who had to be overpowered, put under a cold shower, bound, and dragged to the back. The other combatants retreat and stretch out on benches.

The opening scenes of reported action, five days' worth, have been collapsed and converted into a mime of Achilles, foaming at the mouth, running raving after the alternately somnambulistic and manic, even convulsive, Penthesilea. Two male nurses and the director playing the other three Greek kings regard the chase and comment among themselves inaudibly. The other women and male patients stamp their feet incessantly in the background.

The mime consists of the first glimpse Penthesilea has of Achilles. First blank face, then hot flush followed by a convulsion, at which point the sisters intervene to calm her. When she looks at Achilles, Penthesilea hears nothing, stares drunkenly. Her chasing him is such that it looks as if

hatred drives her. Then she rescues Achilles from death at the hands of a Trojan. He tries to kill her by way of thanks, but she escapes laughing and disappears. The nurses consider chaining Achilles' ankles together to restrain him (due to his foaming at the mouth and raving) but decide against it. They are the force of reason against his mad determination. Finally, he falls into a pool with no water. Penthesilea, blind with rage, tries and fails to climb to his rescue.

Four men play Achilles' horses. This madman, in triumphal entry, beats them with a whip graciously loaned to him by one of the nurses. The patients stamp the earth with their feet.

Her thighs wrapped around the body of her manly horse, Penthesilea catches up to Achilles. He veers, she cuts him off, and racing along side him, strikes murder at him. He swings—she can't stop herself and overshoots him, hits a stone, and FALLS. All the women fall on top of each other making a great heap. Out of this she stands, but even the thought of catching him is stopped dead.

This entire mime takes place before Achilles' first proper entrance. What saves this event from total chaos are the moments of startling immobility, the gestures of falling and standing up. Stillness when the heart is frozen in awe. When Achilles is struck down by the Trojan, Penthesilea goes white *for a full two minutes.*

I cannot accurately convey to you the terror I experienced during these opening minutes. I had no idea what would happen next, and the danger was thrilling. Here in this silent, hidden house of unreason, you have distilled the monster beneath the skin in each and every one of us. It takes madmen to teach us the truth about ourselves. When we first set out together to discover what to do with ourselves in this Napoleonic world, who could have predicted that this is where we would find it.

Achilles enters the central playing area previously occupied by the three Greek kings. He doesn't even know he's been injured. As fellow Kings Odysseus and Diomedes flatter and try to persuade him to leave with them, all he notices is his horse (played by two male patients) sweating. The kings can't get his attention away from thoughts of Penthesilea. He simply stares into the distance. He doesn't hear a word of what these reasonable kings are telling him. All they care about is trapping and forcing Penthesilea to declare allegiance to Greeks or Trojans.

To Achilles, played by an erotomaniac, battle is a heaving bed. Desire and death are whispered in the same breath. He wants her as bride and prized corpse to parade through the streets of Troy. The aptitude the Erotomaniac has for raving suits his role well.

Penthesilea's entrance follows hard. Prothoe, her Princess, is played by a nurse. The Amazon Penthesilea has no bosom, but in the end, she will find the place where the feeling that has beaten her down, that crippled her at the sight of Achilles, is lodged. She will find the killing feeling in the same place.

Her FALL perturbed her mind. The sisters take her to a bench and get her to lie down for the rest of the scene. Achilles hears nothing of what's said to him. Penthesilea can't remember what she's said or done, and doesn't recognize herself in the mirror that is Achilles. They have entered a new world.

Heinrich, I hear you crying out through Penthesilea: a spiteful power always steps in your way as you try to catch hold of FAME. This leads to boiling blood of defiance. Fame is a man with golden locks of hair to catch.

If this were a production in a professional theater, sane men would be behaving madly. Here we have madmen trying and failing to behave sanely. The end result is similar, and the madness of their passion seems the sanest thing in a mad world. Sanest because it carries the most force. At one point, a Greek captured for love by an Amazon asks the other prisoners in an undertone: "Was ever there a dream as mad as what's the truth here?"

Prothoe sees the queen is mad with a violent passion, unfit like a poisoned lion—eyes glittering strongly, thoughts engendered out of night—she's in a fever. Desire makes her ill. So much so, that the nurses have to put her in a cold bath. She can't stop wanting what she can't have, the way she wants to have it. She cannot accept Achilles unless she wins him worthily, with her sword. Ambition will kill her in the end.

The girls on the benches make red paper flowers for the love Feast. Red blood against the white tile. Penthesilea tears the flowers to pieces and the girls pick up the pieces. She tears off her necklace. The pearls roll on the tiles scattered in every direction. The girls try to catch them before they roll down the drains.

Penthesilea bursts into tears when she can't run away from her conqueror. She stares into the sun—Achilles, Fame—the sun with golden locks of fire. Finally she dives into the bath and the nurses have to retrieve her before she drowns herself. She passes out.

These lovers feel like two incompatible forces of nature.

Prothoe says: "How many feelings stir inside a woman's breast that never were intended for the light of day." The enemy lives in her own breast, the enemy that will make her stoop in the end.

Achilles comes unarmed to her, her prisoner. Caught in a dream of loving each other to death, they no longer know who they are. Their love scene is interrupted by the battle. He challenges her to a final duel, thinking he can save her honor by letting her win him. Instead, mad with rage, she comes after him with her madmen dogs to tear him apart.

Sensing disaster, the director orders the attendants to knock down and tie up Achilles, just as the sisters try to do the same to Penthesilea. They manage Achilles, but not Penthesilea, and the director disavows any responsibility for what occurs after.

This Penthesilea actually tears her own flesh with her teeth so as to achieve the effect of bloody mouth and hands. And that's the true sense of the gesture, anyway, that it is herself—and Achilles—she is tearing to pieces with her teeth. She and her lover are one flesh! A horror-stricken pause ensues. Penthesilea stares off into infinity, like a writer at an empty page. The director tears off his glasses, throws them at her, then he begs her forgiveness.

Now practically catatonic, Penthesilea douses herself with bowl after bowl of water, baptizing herself to the realization of her incarceration. She stares at her hands and touches her mouth, tasting the blood. Begins babbling about kissing Achilles dead. Kissing and biting, biting and kissing. Kisses the straitjacketed Achilles one last time. Turns to the platform and speaks directly to us: "I wasn't such a mad one as might seem." Then, before anyone can restrain her, stabs herself four times with a feeling: the more alive she is, the more vulnerable to death. Topples and dies.

I don't know if she was dead or alive, but the idea of her death makes a hole in my life that will never be filled.

F. C. Dahlmann
17 October 1809

+ + +

As regards Karoline, in her letters to me after our fateful meeting that cold day in January, she referred to herself as "he" or "a male friend." Sometime later she suffered a loss of reason as the result of a forbidden romantic attachment. This loss could be directly attributed to her blind surrender to desire coupled with her incapacity to control or moderate her passions—all symptoms of the disease of writing poetry. Eligible bachelors who threw her over gave way to a married academic who ultimately chose his wife over her, over a ménage à trois, over a suicide pact. This rupture provided the catalyst for the suicide, but the groundwork was laid long before. She played the scene somewhat differently than the way we had rehearsed it. Standing on the banks of that same river, on July 26, 1806, she filled her shawl with rocks, and stabbed herself twice in the heart with a dagger. So she had the strength after all. Her desire to travel was finally, if posthumously, fulfilled.

> He who has felt the deepest of all
> wounds in mind and heart:
> the bitter call to part;
> he who loved what's lost, elected
> to relinquish the selected
> beloved heart.
>
> (FROM *THE ONE LAMENT*, BY KAROLINE VON GÜNDERRODE)

+ + +

Just as love is desiring what Kleist does not have, writing his life means he must disappear.

On the last night, calmly and firmly, he burns all documents and letters. He makes arrangements for his barber to be paid and a gift given to his landlord. Then he sleeps soundly, knowing that his death will be worthy of Cato, the man of Utica.

Henriette is his lover in the most glorious and sensual of deaths. When they cut him open they know him, as they feel his liver enlarged from too much alcohol, as the bile spills black on the white sheet. Henriette had dressed for him that morning, her nude body white as goose down, soft and feathery, the lace and ribbons, but he never touched her, because he would not sully her purity with his inky stains. They cut into the cancer in her womb; she was riddled with lumps. He never touched her, he never wanted her that way. When she played the piano, he felt her playing his body, and the sensation was ethereal, blasting him with the white light of the sun: it was Penthesilea seeing Achilles for the first time, blinded by his force.

The love of Kleist and Henriette Vogel is at last fully realized in the performance of murder-suicide, the artist finding in Vogel someone to push him ever sunward, toward the creative act unmediated, actualization in the flesh of the theatrical juncture of Penthesilea and Achilles—an eclipse of opposing forces blotting each other out completely for all eternity. Kleist's art finds its perfect incarnation in this criminal act. And then it's over, the rotting flesh on the tables left behind for the relatives to try to recognize, but the bodies are transformed.

Kleist believed that with this act wings would erupt from his shoulder blades, that he would begin to live in a place of billowing green fields, where the air is thinner, where we love with the love of angels.

At that moment I was somehow able to understand the extraordinary phrase that "time shall be no more." Probably . . . it's the same second in which the jug of water overturned by the epileptic Muhammad did not have time to spill, while he had time during the same second to survey all the dwellings of Allah.

DOSTOEVSKY, *THE IDIOT*

CODA

And so to finish off this collection of dialogues, the reader may imagine a final dialogue between Heinrich von Kleist and Mohamed Atta, between the artist-suicide and the suicide pilot. And try to imagine an understanding (because we cannot truly understand) as to why and how the impulse to create transgressive art and the impulse to commit violence lie so perilously close to each other.

When Atta asks Kleist why he did it, Kleist tells him: Henriette and I sit down to face each other in the shallow trench. After she presses her white kid-gloved hands together in her lap, I inflict death on her beneath her left breast with the large pistol (she falls backward and faces up), and lay the weapon at the edge of the trench. Then I place the not quite fully loaded (did I make a mistake?) small pistol in my mouth, because this is where my voice originates—a third pistol is on the table a mere eight paces away in case I really do make a mistake—and inflict death on myself. In the same second, I drop the pistol at my feet, rest my hands on my knees, and feeling the one-third-ounce piece of lead impact the bone behind my uvula, I clench my teeth so tightly, they will need an iron lever to pry my mouth open to find the cause imbedded in my brain, because I have nothing more to say. From the moment she and I sit down together, I know I am dying and my vision is complete.

Atta tells Kleist: In the instant the nose (not the wing) of the plane touches the tower I have time to travel to Jerusalem, rise into the seven heavens where I speak with angels, prophets, and Allah, visit the fiery Gehenna, and return in time for my obliteration. I have no desire outside of this moment. We concur that the end of time is all.

And in the reader's speculation concerning the twin motivations of the artist and the terrorist, he may turn to Wallace Stevens's characterization of the imaginative process as knowing "desire without an object of desire." Because the object of desire is the doing and only the doing of the act itself, the experience of desire is its own object. Any object of desire existing outside the act of desire is an illusion. "All mind and violence and nothing felt." So much for wings, green fields, thin air, and love. So much for the undoing of governments, societies, and regimes. Any response of any audience is posthumous and unknowable. In the doing itself they survey "all the dwellings of Allah" and "know everything."

A SHORT BIBLIOGRAPHY

Over the years we've read a fair amount of the scholarship on the writers that we've taken up. We list here only those few books and articles that made immediate impact on our various chapters. We've not listed work, primary or secondary, cited in the text; for such work, see "Works Cited."

Groundzeroland

Cardwell, Diane. "A Nation Challenged: Ground Zero; First Viewing Platform Opens to the Public." *New York Times,* December 30, 2001, sec. 1B, 8.

Chen, David W. "Office Workers Haunted by Views of Terror Site." *New York Times,* January 19, 2002, A1.

Collins, Glenn. "Vessels of a City's Grief; Displays from Sept. 11 Form a Museum Exhibition." *New York Times,* March 8, 2002, B1.

Cooper, Michael. "A Nation Challenged: The Site; a Viewing Stand Brings Pilgrims to Ground Zero." *New York Times,* December 31, 2001, B5.

———. "Metro Briefing/New York: Manhattan: Tickets for Ground Zero." *New York Times,* January 9, 2002, B4.

Dewan, Shaila K. "Blue Halo Suggested for Wound Downtown." *New York Times,* January 2, 2002, B3.

Feuer, Alan. "Video Captures Sept. 11 Horror in Raw Replay." *New York Times,* January 12, 2002, 1.

Handelman, David. "History's Rough Draft in a Map of Ground Zero." *New York Times,* January 3, 2002, F9.

Koestenbaum, Wayne. *Andy Warhol.* New York: Viking Penguin, 2001.

Leland, John. "Letting the View Speak for Itself." *New York Times,* January 3, 2002, F1.
Lipton, Eric, and James Glanz. "A Nation Challenged: Relics; from the Rubble, Artifacts of Anguish." *New York Times,* January 27, 2002, sec. 1, 1.
Murphy, Dean E. "As Public Yearns to See Ground Zero, Survivors Call a Viewing Stand Ghoulish." *New York Times,* January 13, 2002, sec. 1, 31.
Osborne, William. "Symphony Orchestras and Artist-Prophets: Cultural Isomorphism and the Allocation of Power in Music." *Leonardo Music Journal* 9 (1999): 69–75.
Rich, Frank. "Patriotism on the Cheap." *New York Times* (Op-Ed), January 5, 2002, A11.
Robinson, Marc. *The Other American Drama.* Baltimore and London: Johns Hopkins University Press, 1997.
Saulny, Susan. "A Nation Challenged: Tourism; Pilgrimage to New York City: Paying Respects and Spending Little." *New York Times,* December 29, 2001, B1.
Stewart, Barbara. "Crowds Line up for New Ground Zero View." *New York Times,* January 2, 2002, B3.

Literary Terrorists
Caws, Mary Ann. *Joseph Cornell's Theater of the Mind.* New York: Thames & Hudson, 1993.
Douglas, John, and Mark Olshaker. *Unabomber: On the Trail of America's Most-Wanted Serial Killer.* New York: Pocket Books, 1996.
Gibbs, Nancy, Richard Lacayo, Lance Morrow, Jill Smolowe, and David Van Biema. *Mad Genius.* New York: Warner Books, 1996.
Lentricchia, Frank, ed. *Introducing Don DeLillo.* Durham, N.C., and London: Duke University Press, 1991.
McShane, Kynosta, ed. *Joseph Cornell.* New York: Museum of Modern Art, 1980.

Solitary Savages
Barnes, Anne. "Disgusting Designer Label Litero Nasty." *London Times,* April 25, 1991, Features.
Bean, Henry. "Slayground." Review of *American Psycho,* by Bret Easton Ellis. *Los Angeles Times,* March 17, 1991, Book Review Desk, 1.
Billington, James H. *The Icon and the Axe.* New York: Random House, 1966.
Brombert, Victor. *In Praise of Antiheroes.* Chicago: University of Chicago Press, 1999.
Humphrey, Clark. "Psychological Horrors—Two Novels Embody Current Murder Cycle." *Seattle Times,* April 28, 1991, L7.
Kelly, Mary Pat, ed. *Martin Scorsese: A Journey.* New York: Thunder Mouth Press, 1991.
Kennedy, Paul. "*American Psycho*—Sick or Creative?" *Florida Today,* July 3, 1991.
Lehmann-Haupt, Christopher. "Books of the Times; 'Psycho': Whither Death without Life?" *New York Times,* March 11, 1991, C18.
Marchand, Philip. "*American Psycho* Storm Rages: Gruesome Novel Sparks Debate about Literature, Censorship, and Media Hype." *Toronto Star,* April 13, 1991, G3.
Porlock, Harvey. "On the Critical List." *London Times,* March 24, 1991, Features.
———. "On the Critical List." *London Times,* April 28, 1991, Features.
Rosenblatt, Roger. "Snuff This Book! Will Bret Easton Ellis Get Away with Murder?" *New York Times,* December 16, 1990, sec. 7, 3.

Sion, Michael. "*American Psycho* Is Just a Book about the 1980s, Author Says." *Reno-Gazette-Journal,* March 20, 1991.
Weinraub, Bernard. "Mailer Tells a Lot: Not All, but a Lot." *New York Times,* October 4, 2000, B1.
Yardley, Jonathan. "'American Psycho': Essence of Trash." *Washington Post,* February 27, 1991, B1.

Crossing the Line

Achebe, Chinua. "An Image of Africa: Racism in Conrad's *Heart of Darkness.*" In *Heart of Darkness: An Authoritative Text, Backgrounds and Sources, Criticism,* ed. Robert Kimbrough. New York: W. W. Norton, 1988.
Canby, V. "From 30's porn to 70's corn." *New York Times,* March 7, 1976, sec. 2.
Cassavetes, John. "What's Wrong with Hollywood." *Film Culture,* no. 19 (1959), 4–5.
———. "Interview." By Jonas Mekas. *Village Voice* (December 23, 1971), 63–64.
———. "Interview." By John Cassavetes. *Film Comment* (July–August 1988).
Combs, Richard. "The Killing of a Chinese Bookie." *Sight and Sound* (winter 1976–77), 61.
Conrad, Joseph. "To Make You See," In *Heart of Darkness: An Authoritative Text, Backgrounds and Sources, Criticism,* ed. Robert Kimbrough. New York: W. W. Norton, 1988.
Di Piero, W. S. "Inspired Muleheadedness." *Take One* 5, no. 3 (August 1976), 35–36.
Dorall, E. N. "Conrad and Coppola: Different Centres of Darkness." In *Heart of Darkness: An Authoritative Text, Backgrounds and Sources, Criticism,* ed. Robert Kimbrough. New York: W. W. Norton, 1988.
Gelmis, Joseph. *The Director as Superstar.* New York: Doubleday, 1970.
Hagen, William M. "*Heart of Darkness* and the Process of *Apocalypse Now.*" In *Heart of Darkness: An Authoritative Text, Backgrounds and Sources, Criticism,* ed. Robert Kimbrough. New York: W. W. Norton, 1988.
Hatch, R. "Films." *Nation* (February 28, 1976), 253–54.
Izenberg, Gerald N. *Modernism and Masculinity.* Chicago: University of Chicago Press, 2000.
LaBrasca, Robert. "Two Visions of 'The horror!'" In *Heart of Darkness: An Authoritative Text, Backgrounds and Sources, Criticism,* ed. Robert Kimbrough. New York: W. W. Norton, 1988.
Levich, Jacob. "John Cassavetes: An American Maverick." *Cineaste* 20, no. 2 (December 1993), 51–53.
LoBrutto, Vincent. "John Cassavetes." *Films in Review* (January–February 1997), 6–10.
Pym, John. "The Killing of a Chinese Bookie." *Monthly Film Bulletin* 47, no. 556 (May 1980): 92.
Sacharov, Al. *The Red Head Book.* New York: Word of Mouth Press, 1982.
Said, Edward W. *Orientalism.* New York: Pantheon Books, 1978.
Sterritt, David, ed. *Jean-Luc Godard: Interviews.* Jackson: University Press of Mississippi, 1998.
Stevenson, James. "John Cassavetes: Film's Bad Boy." *American Film* (January–February 1980), 44–79.
Thomson, David. "'Apocalypse' Then and Now." *New York Times,* Sunday May 13, 2001, 2A1.

Wilmington, Mike. "Worth the Wait: *Apocalypse Now.*" In *Heart of Darkness: An Authoritative Text, Backgrounds and Sources, Criticism,* ed. Robert Kimbrough. New York: W. W. Norton, 1988.

Rough Trade

Brustein, Robert. *The Theatre of Revolt: An Approach to the Modern Drama.* Boston: Little, Brown, 1964.

Coe, Richard N. *The Vision of Jean Genet.* New York: Grove, 1969.

Gates, Henry Louis Jr. *New York Times Book Review,* June 2, 2002, 18.

Soledad Brother: The Prison Letters of George Jackson. Introduction by Jean Genet. New York: Coward McCann, 1970.

Deliberate Orphans

Honegger, Gitta. *Thomas Bernhard: The Making of an Austrian.* New Haven, Conn.: Yale University Press, 2001.

Kiberd, Declan. *Inventing Ireland: The Literature of the Modern Nation.* London: Jonathan Lape, 1995.

Marx, Leo. "Melville's 'Parable of the Walls.'" *Sewanee Review* 61 (1953): 602–27.

Robertson-Lorant, Laurie. *Melville: A Biography.* New York: Clarkson Potter, 1996.

The Last Maniacal Folly of Heinrich von Kleist (A Fiction)

Beckett, Samuel. *Krapp's Last Tape.* New York: Grove Press, 1960.

Geary, John, *Heinrich von Kleist.* Philadelphia: University of Pennsylvania Press, 1968.

Goethe, Johann Wolfgang von. *The Sorrows of Young Werther.* Translated by Michael Hulse. London: Penguin, 1989.

Greenberg, Martin, trans. *Heinrich von Kleist: Five Plays.* New Haven, Conn., and London: Yale University Press, 1988.

Kleist, Heinrich von. *Marquise of O and Other Stories.* Translated by David Luke and Nigel Reeves. Harmondsworth: Penguin, 1978.

Miller, Philip B., ed. *An Abyss Deep Enough: Letters of Heinrich von Kleist.* New York: E. P. Dutton, 1982.

WORKS CITED

Abbott, Jack Henry. *In the Belly of the Beast: Letters from Prison.* New York: Random House, 1981.

Aristotle's "Poetics." Introduction by Francis Fergusson. New York: Hill & Wang, 1961.

Balzac, Honoré de. *Le père Goriot.* New York: C. Scribner's Sons, 1928.

Barthes, Roland. *On Racine.* Translated by Richard Howard. New York: Hill & Wang, 1964.

Bernhard, Thomas. *Old Masters.* Translated by Ewald Osers. London: Quartet Books, 1989.

———. *Wittgenstein's Nephew.* Translated by David McLintock. New York: Alfred A. Knopf, 1989.

———. *Heldenplatz.* Translated by Gitta Honegger. *Conjunctions,* no. 33 (fall 1999).

Bingham, Caleb. *The Columbian Orator.* Boston: J. H. A. Frost, 1841.

Bowles, Paul. *The Sheltering Sky.* New York: New Directions, 1949.

Brandt, George W. *Modern Theories of Drama.* Oxford: Oxford University Press, 1998.

Breton, André. *Manifestoes of Surrealism.* Translated by Richard Seaver. Ann Arbor: University of Michigan Press, 1969.

Burgess, Anthony. *A Clockwork Orange.* New York: W. W. Norton, 1963.

Capote, Truman. *In Cold Blood.* New York: Random House, 1965.

Carlson, Marvin. *Performance: A Critical Introduction.* London and New York: Routledge, 1996. [For material on Chris Burden and Robert Wilson.]

Cassavetes, John. *Shadows.* 1961.

———. *A Child Is Waiting.* 1962.

———. *The Killing of a Chinese Bookie.* 1976.

———. *Opening Night.* 1978.
Chekhov, Anton. "The Cherry Orchard." In *The Plays of Anton Chekhov.* Translated by Paul Schmidt. New York: Harper Collins, 1997.
Conrad, Joseph. *Heart of Darkness.* New York: W. W. Norton, 1988.
Coppola, Francis Ford. *Apocalypse Now.* 1979. *Apocalypse Now Redux.* 2001.
DeLillo, Don. *The Names.* New York: Alfred A. Knopf, 1982.
———. *White Noise.* New York: Viking, 1985.
———. *Libra.* New York: Viking, 1988.
———. *Mao II.* New York: Viking, 1991.
Dostoevsky, Fyodor. *Crime and Punishment.* Translated by Richard Pevear and Larissa Volokhonsky. New York: Vintage Classics, 1993.
———. *Notes from Underground.* Translated by Richard Pevear and Larissa Volokhonsky. New York: Vintage Classics, 1993.
———. *The Idiot.* Translated by Richard Pevear and Larissa Volokhonsky. New York: Knopf, 2001.
Douglass, Frederick. *Narrative of the Life of Frederick Douglass, an American Slave.* New York: Modern Library, 2000.
Eliot, T. S. *Selected Essays.* New York: Harcourt, Brace & World, 1960.
———. *Collected Poems, 1909–1962.* New York: Harcourt Brace Jovanovich, 1964.
Ellis, Bret Easton. *American Psycho.* New York: Vintage Contemporaries, 1991.
Fitzgerald, F. Scott. *The Great Gatsby.* New York: Charles Scribner's Sons, 1925.
Frank, Joseph. *Dostoevsky: The Miraculous Years, 1865–1871.* Princeton, N.J.: Princeton University Press, 1976.
———. *Dostoevsky: The Stir of Liberation, 1860–1865.* Princeton, N.J.: Princeton University Press, 1986.
Frost, Robert. *Selected Letters of Robert Frost.* Edited by Lawrence Thompson. New York: Holt, Rinehart & Winston, 1964.
Genet, Jean. *The Maids and Deathwatch.* Translated by Bernard Frechtman. New York: Grove Press, 1954.
———. *The Balcony.* Translated by Bernard Frechtman. New York: Grove Press, 1958.
———. *The Blacks: A Clown Show.* Translated by Bernard Frechtman. New York: Grove Press, 1960.
———. *The Screens.* Translated by Bernard Frechtman. New York: Grove Press, 1962.
———. *Our Lady of the Flowers.* Translated by Bernard Frechtman. New York: Grove Press, 1963.
Kaczynski, Theodore. *The Unabomber Manifesto: Industrial Society and Its Future.* Berkeley: Jolly Roger Press, 1995.
Lang, Fritz. *M.* 1931.
Lish, Gordon. *Dear Mr. Capote.* New York: Holt, Rinehart & Winston, 1983.
Mailer, Norman. *The Executioner's Song.* Boston: Little, Brown & Co., 1979.
Mann, Thomas. *Death in Venice and Seven Other Stories.* Translated by H. T. Lowe-Porter. New York: Vintage International, 1989.
Melville, Herman. *Moby-Dick.* Edited by Charles Feidelson, Jr. Indianapolis: Bobbs-Merrill, 1964.
———. *Pierre.* Evanston, Ill.: Northwestern University Press; Chicago: Newberry Library, 1971.
———. "Bartleby the Scrivener, a Story of Wall Street." In *The Piazza Tales and Other Prose Pieces, 1839–1860.* Edited by Harrison Hayford, Alma A. MacDougall,

G. Thomas Tanselle, et al. Evanston, Ill.: Northwestern University Press; Chicago: Newberry Library, 1987.
———. *Correspondence*. Edited by Lynn Horth. Evanston, Ill.: Northwestern University Press; Chicago: Newberry Library, 1993.
O'Neill, Eugene. *The Iceman Cometh*. New York: Random House, 1967.
Ozick, Cynthia. "Dostoyevsky's Unabomber." *New Yorker*, February 24–March 3, 1997.
Pound, Ezra. *Literary Essays of Ezra Pound*. Edited by T. S. Eliot. New York: New Directions, 1968.
Scorsese, Martin. *Mean Streets*. 1974.
———. *Taxi Driver*. 1977.
———. *The King of Comedy*. 1983.
Scott, Sir Walter. *The Lady of the Lake*. London: Blackie & Son, n.d.
Shelley, Mary. *Frankenstein*. Middlesex: Penguin Books, 1985.
Shelley, Percy. "A Defence of Poetry." In *Criticism: The Major Texts*. Edited by Walter Jackson Bate. New York: Harcourt Brace Jovanovich, 1970.
Sterritt, David. *Jean-Luc Godard: Interviews*. Jackson: University Press of Mississippi, 1998.
Stevens, Wallace. *The Collected Poems*. New York: Random House, 1982.
Stockhausen, Karlheinz. "Karlheinz Stockhausen." (http://www.stockhausen.org.)
Synge, J. M. *"The Playboy of the Western World" and "Riders to the Sea."* New York: Dover Publications, 1993.
Tommasini, Anthony. "The Devil Made Him Do It." *New York Times*, September 30, 2001.
Von Kleist, Heinrich. *Plays*. Translated by Humphrey Trevelyan. New York: Continuum, 1982.
———. *Five Plays*. Translated by Martin Greenberg. New Haven, Conn., and London: Yale University Press, 1988.
White, Edmund. *Genet: A Biography*. New York: Vintage, 1994.
Williams, Tennessee. *A Streetcar Named Desire*. New York: New Directions, 1947.
Wordsworth, William. "Preface to the Second Edition of Lyrical Ballads." In *Criticism: The Major Texts*. Edited by Walter Jackson Bate. New York: Harcourt Brace Jovanovich, 1970.
Yeats, W. B. *Selected Poems and Three Plays*. Edited by M. L. Rosenthal. New York: Macmillan, 1986.

ACKNOWLEDGMENTS

We're grateful for the reactions to the manuscript given to us by Edna Andrews, Don DeLillo, Andrew DuBois, Tom Ferraro, Derek Goldman, Fredric Jameson, Scott Lindroth (who also led us to the Stockhausen controversy), Marlane Meyer, and John Rowe. Stanley Kauffmann read the entire text with his unique and bracing combination of no-holds-barred criticism, generosity, and encouragement. Words are inadequate to say precisely how much we admire his way as an educator—a way now pretty much out of favor, and feared, in U.S. schools, especially in institutions of higher learning. Grievous loss for all who would teach and learn. Frank Lentricchia wishes to thank Jody McAuliffe: the idea of this book is hers.

INDEX